Everyday Maths
through Everyday Provision

Children are born naturally mathematical, so why is it sometimes so difficult to observe children being mathematical? Why do so many of us think we are 'bad' at maths and how does this subconsciously affect the provision, experiences and opportunities we provide for young children who are starting their mathematical learning journey?

This easily accessible book will help you to realise the wonderful mathematical learning happening in your setting all day and every day through the familiar resources and experiences routinely offered to young children. It will help you to think more reflectively about what you are providing for children and suggest ways of making provision richer and more exciting for you and the children in your care.

With chapters linked to areas of continuous provision including sand, water, dough, role play, music, outdoors and ICT among many others, this book features:

- a wide range of activities including key questions, vocabulary and advice on observations
- lists of key resources
- ideas to support children's mathematical mark making
- useful links to stories and rhymes to engage children and promote mathematical learning
- links to other areas of learning and development
- suggestions for involving parents.

Providing a wealth of exciting, meaningful, play-based ways to promote mathematical learning and create a maths-rich environment, this highly practical book will help you to develop young children's confidence and enjoyment of maths through your everyday provision. It is a perfect resource for Early Years Practitioners working in all settings, as well as those studying on Childcare, Early Childhood and Early Years Professional Status courses.

Elaine Bennett is an experienced Early Years/Key Stage 1 practitioner and freelance writer who has also worked as an Early Years Consultant for Southend Local Authority.

Jenny Weidner is an Advanced Skills Teacher specialising in mathematics and provides training for professionals working in the Foundation Stage and Key Stage 1.

Everyday Maths through Everyday Provision

Developing opportunities for mathematics in the early years

Elaine Bennett
and
Jenny Weidner

Routledge
Taylor & Francis Group

LONDON AND NEW YORK

First published 2012
by Routledge
2 Park Square, Milton Park, Abingdon, Oxon OX14 4RN

Simultaneously published in the USA and Canada
by Routledge
711 Third Avenue, New York, NY 10017

Routledge is an imprint of the Taylor & Francis Group, an informa business

British Library Cataloguing in Publication Data
A catalogue record for this book is available from the British Library

Library of Congress Cataloging in Publication Data
Bennett, Elaine.
Everyday maths through everyday provision : developing opportunities for mathematics
in the early years / Elaine Bennett and Jenny Weidner.
p. cm.
Includes bibliographical references.
1. Mathematics--Study and teaching (Early childhood) 2. Early childhood education.
I. Weidner, Jenny. II. Title.
QA135.6.B4675 2011
372.7--dc23
2011024760

ISBN: 978-0-415-66435-6 (hbk)
ISBN: 978-0-415-66436-3 (pbk)
ISBN: 978-0-203-81885-5 (ebk)

Typeset in Optima
by Saxon Graphics Ltd, Derby

Printed and bound in Great Britain by
TJ International Ltd, Padstow, Cornwall

Contents

Acknowledgements

We would like to thank Annamarie Kino for sharing in our vision on this project and her many words of wisdom and advice along the way. Our thanks also go to Sir Peter Williams for not only his work which has inspired us, but also his passion for Early Years Education and his willingness to write our Foreword, for which we are extremely grateful.

We also send our thanks to the staff and children at Earls Hall Pre-School and Earls Hall Infant School, Westcliff-on-Sea and Richmond Avenue Primary School in Southend, Essex, for their involvement and support. A special mention goes to Sue Westmore, EYFS Adviser and practitioner, a dedicated Early Years advocate and great friend, who works tirelessly to promote exciting and inspiring learning opportunities for all children, whatever the weather.

A final very special thank you goes to our families who continue to provide the love and support (and peace and quiet) that enable us to follow our ambitions. We are eternally grateful!

Foreword

When I was asked in 2007 by the then Secretary of State at the Department for Children, Schools and Families to review the teaching of mathematics in Primary Schools and in Early Years Settings, I had little idea of what the task might entail. Happily, I was supported by an experienced and enlightened advisory committee and by an excellent team in the department.

In setting out on what became the 'Williams Review', an early focus was on key stages 2 and 3 in Primary and the need, as I saw it, for confident teachers to take children's learning forward. Confident teachers, I reasoned, would instil confidence in their pupils. But what became rapidly clear to all of us involved was that this learning process in Primary depended to a very great extent on the degree to which even younger children were comfortable with number and counting from a much earlier age. The EYFS Framework had of course recently been published and the importance of early learning in mathematics was becoming widely recognised.

But how, we asked ourselves, could this process of early learning from birth to five years of age be helped? Perhaps unsurprisingly, what was apparent in virtually every EYFS setting we visited was that the answer to this question involved confidence developed through the medium of play and indeed I stressed this in my final report. All well and good, but warm words are of little help to an Early Years practitioner. More practical support is needed.

That is why this resource is so important. What Elaine and Jenny stress so persuasively is that young children are naturally mathematical and that the settings in which they begin to learn are filled with mathematical symbolism in their everyday activities and experiences. It is an intensely practical book which will be of enormous help to practitioners, not only in helping them plan resources and activities, but equally importantly in reflecting on their own approach to mathematical learning.

Sir Peter Williams

Introduction

Maths is all around

The world we live in is full of mathematics, from the numbers on our doors, to the times in our television guides or the numbers on our mobile phones. Humans are born mathematical, with even the youngest babies showing mathematical awareness, and yet in this world rich in maths, why do so many adults feel intimidated by the mere mention of the subject?

Reflecting on our own education, mathematics lessons consisted of pages of workbooks to be completed, long and complicated irrelevant problems to solve, and formal rote teaching with little, if any, practical activities. Answers were either right or wrong. The *Independent Review of Mathematics Teaching in Early Years Settings and Primary Schools* conducted by Sir Peter Williams (2008) highlighted the importance of practical approaches to maths to develop confident young mathematicians who use and apply maths in their everyday lives.

In terms of the Early Years setting, how does our own personal experience of mathematics affect the provision we offer to the children in our care? Do we teach them that it's good to take risks, it's okay to get things wrong and it's important to learn from mistakes? Or is maths seen as a subject that is difficult and has set right or wrong answers?

This book aims to demonstrate that maths is in fact inherent in the Early Years setting, in the resources we provide, the everyday daily routines and in children's natural self-initiated play. It is therefore crucial to instil in our children that maths is all around them; it involves them and is an important part of their daily lives. As practitioners we need to ensure that our approach towards maths reflects the notion that it is purposeful, meaningful and relevant. We need to recognise and celebrate the maths that is naturally occurring within our settings all day, everyday, inside and out.

Developing a maths-rich environment

Considering your own setting, reflect upon how maths 'happens' within the environment. Do you merely have a well-stocked 'maths area', consisting of a range of commercial equipment, which gives the impression that maths only happens in this area? Are children told 'Go to the maths area!'? If so, what ideas will children form about maths? Instead are they encouraged to use this equipment in other areas of provision as and when they need it, for example taking buttons or shells into the sand tray or calculators into the shop? This helps them to make links across areas of learning and realise that the skills they are developing are transferable.

A maths-rich environment should encourage children to use and apply their mathematical knowledge, skills and understanding across the areas of provision, whether in the water tray, in the home corner or whilst working with dough. The activities within this book aim to promote and support children's use of maths through their everyday play.

Working together: involving parents and carers

Just as many practitioners feel less than confident about mathematics, it would be fair to say that many parents and carers share the same feelings. We all recognise the importance of working with families as children's most influential educators and for maths in particular this is essential. It is vital to share the positive experiences and learning opportunities you are providing in maths within your setting to ensure families support this ethos at home. There are many different ways to build links with children's home lives with regard to early mathematics. Ideas such as lending out games and puzzles, having a 'maths' open morning where families can join in with activities and offering workshops to help families recognise maths that happens in everyday lives can all work towards dispelling the myth of maths as something threatening and scary!

The importance of observation, assessment and planning

As practitioners we need to reflect on how we plan and assess maths within our settings. Planning should always come from the needs and interests of the children within our care, making planning weeks ahead in advance irrelevant and meaningless. Planning can and should change on a day to day basis and we should not be afraid to cross out and adapt our plans in light of what we have seen and heard. We need to consider how maths appears in our planning. Is maths only a separate box on a planning sheet or does it feature in continuous provision plans, running throughout the activities and resources on offer? In terms of assessment and observation, are children sat and quizzed about numbers and shapes which are then ticked off on a worksheet or list? Or are we observing them when engaged in self-initiated play, tackling problems in real-life, purposeful contexts? This book aims to support you to plan for maths throughout areas of provision and ideas for assessment and observation. You will see these prompts referred to as 'Look, listen and note', a heading we took from the EYFS (DCSF 2008) which sums up an effective approach towards assessment.

How to use this book

- This book consists of 12 chapters, each relating to a specific area of provision. Chapters follow the same format and all consist of:
  - An introduction explaining the importance of the area
  - Links to other areas of learning (linked to proposed areas of learning as identified in Dame Clare Tickell's review 2011)
  - Key resources
  - Maths web
  - Main activities
  - Look, listen and note
  - Key questions
  - Key vocabulary
  - Health and safety
  - Useful stories and rhymes
  - Links to theory
  - Making mathematical marks
- This book is not intended to be followed as a rigid scheme and activities are not ordered in levels of difficulty. They are designed for practitioners to dip into and provide starting points for learning across the areas of provision, and they should be adapted to suit the children's needs and interests.
- Main activities are designed to be adult-led activities with ideas to take the activity further in the 'What next' section that follows.
- The key questions and vocabulary suggestions are not prescriptive or exhaustive lists. Instead they provide ideas of language and questions that could be modelled with children to develop their vocabulary and understanding. The key vocabulary

suggestions have been created in reference to the *Mathematical Vocabulary* booklet word list for Reception (DFEE 2000).

- The 'Making mathematical marks' section was largely influenced by Sir Peter Williams's findings (2008), that children need more opportunities to record their early mathematical thinking. This does not merely mean recording sums, but relates to opportunities for children to make meaningful representations about their own maths.

- Links to theory have been provided to underpin the importance of each type of provision; however, more practical advice is offered in the following 'What does this look like in practice?'

- Education is a continually evolving entity and although we have referred to government documentation this book is not dependent upon any set framework but is instead based upon sound early years pedagogy and effective practice.

We hope that this book provides you with some food for thought as a useful starting point for embedding mathematics within your own setting, from the home corner, to the sand tray and out into the garden. There is a wealth of excellent practice in Early Years settings today. Our aim is to ensure that all children have the opportunity to become confident and excited mathematicians, inspired by practitioners who are positive 'mathematical role models' and enjoy playing with maths!

1 Water

Why water is important

Water offers numerous opportunities across all areas of learning. Children have a natural fascination with water and it can provide some of the most exciting and exhilarating types of play. All children have some experience of water in their lives whether it's through swimming, visits to the beach, washing up, drinking, bath time, rain or splashing in puddles. It is in fact one of the only resources in the setting that every child will undoubtedly have had some experience of. They will already have created their own ideas about capacity and will enjoy exploring these ideas further when working in the water tray, using buckets of water in the outdoor area or squirty bottles and hoses. The language that children will use in this area of provision will be rich and varied when modelled and supported by adults.

Links to other areas of learning

Personal Social and Emotional Development	• Developing independence by choosing and using a range of tools and equipment • Developing self-care by putting on wellies and coats for outdoor use • Working as a group, negotiating plans and the use of equipment • Opportunities for sustained play for long periods of time, particularly in the outdoor area

Communication and Language	• Water words such as drip, splash, drop, splosh • Imaginative play involving themes such as underwater adventures, bath time and seaside • Talking about ideas and plans when using water and negotiating with others about resources and equipment to use
Literacy	• Stories and rhymes about water • Using water pots with brushes to write letters and words in the outdoor area or on large paper
Understanding the World	• Investigating water and its properties using all the senses • Finding out about weather and the impact it has on the local area or wider world • The importance of water for growing plants, fruit and vegetables; investigating the effect on plants if they have no water, for example using cress, beans or sunflowers • Exploring floating and sinking on large and small scales; linking this to boats and travelling on water • Investigating forces, for example ways of moving water using water wheels or pipettes • Identifying the uses of water in our world, for example for washing and cleaning, and including religious links such as baptism • Religious stories from the Bible such as Noah's Ark
Physical Development	• Using a range of tools and equipment when exploring water in the water tray or outdoor area • Talking about the role of water to keep us healthy, including drinking water, cleaning teeth and hand washing • Developing fine motor skills by using equipment such as pipettes or brushes with water
Expressive Arts and Design	• Songs and rhymes linked to water • Small world play contexts linked to water such as the seaside or underwater • Painting with water or using watercolour paints on different types of paper • Mixing colours in puddles or in the water tray using food colouring • Rain sounds and water sounds using instruments such as shakers, rain sticks and tambourines

Mathematics	• Capacity
	• Shape
	• Number
	• Counting
	• Calculating

Key resources

- Empty bottles and containers
- Buckets
- Funnels
- Tubes
- Guttering
- Pipes
- Pipettes and syringes for sucking up water and squirting
- Pots with holes
- Measuring cylinders, jugs and spoons
- Water wheels
- Bubbles
- Various sized brushes
- Cups
- Wellington boots and rain-proof clothing
- Sponges and cloths
- Food colouring
- Nets

Maths web

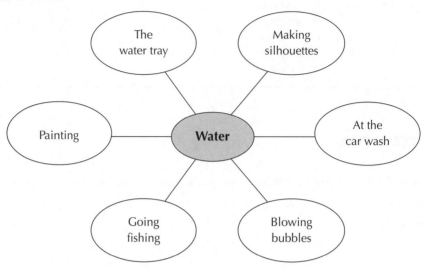

Making silhouettes

Explain that the water tray resources keep getting mixed up. Can the children think of a way of organising them? Allow time to explore sorting the equipment and note children's choices. What is the same about each piece of equipment? What is different? Can the children make a record of the equipment that is in the water tray? Talk about how they can use this to check whether any items are missing or if the correct number of items are in the tray. Work with the children to create a silhouette plan of each piece of equipment by drawing around the base of each. Can the children match each container or resource to its silhouette image? When the plan is being made talk about organising the equipment into the order of containers that hold the least to those that hold the most water.

At the car wash

Explain that the cars and bikes in the outdoor area are very dirty and need to be cleaned. Ask the children to help. Talk to them about what they will need, for example buckets, sponges, water and hoses. Discuss the idea of not wasting water so they need to be careful how much they use. How much water do they think it will take to wash one car? Two cars? How many cars could they wash with 5 buckets of water? Test out their ideas. Provide a range of differently sized buckets and explore their ideas about which holds more or less by using them to wash small cars or bikes. How many small buckets of water are needed? Is this more or less than the number of tall buckets/wide buckets? Encourage children to label the cars with how many buckets of water were needed to wash them using chalks on the floor in the outdoor area.

Blowing bubbles

Work with children to make a bubble mixture by mixing washing up liquid with water. Use small bubble wands from bubble bottles to practise blowing bubbles. Can they describe the bubbles that they blow using mathematical language to identify their size and shape? Set challenges for children with bottles of bubbles, such as who can blow 10 bubbles exactly? Who can blow the biggest/smallest bubble? Who can blow bubbles to travel over the wall? Once children have explored bottles of bubbles, talk about how to make different-shaped bubbles using new wands. Use thin wire with the children to make new shapes such as triangles and squares for larger bubble wands. Put these wands into the bubble mixture to coat the wand and then wave them through the air. What shape are the bubbles? Are all the bubbles the same or are they different?

Going fishing

Place a range of different-coloured objects in the water tray. Provide children with a variety of coloured buckets (matching the colours of the objects). Explain that the children are going fishing. Give them a range of different-sized nets and allow them to have time to fish for the objects; note whether they choose to sort the objects using the coloured buckets. Prompt children to sort the objects by colour, using the buckets if they do not choose to after time exploring. Pose questions to extend children's learning, such as, can they find out how many of each colour object there are? Can they record this to label each coloured bucket? Which colour has the most/least objects? If there was one more red/yellow object how many would there be? How many red and yellow objects are there altogether?

Painting

Use chalks with the children to draw shapes or write numerals in the outside area. Give each child an empty paint pot and ask each to fill the pot, for example 'half full', 'nearly full' or 'full'. Can they fill the pots correctly? Provide each child with a paint brush and allow time to make marks using the brushes, matching the shapes and numbers made with chalks. Can they wash the chalk shapes or numerals away by tracing over them using the water? Who can draw 5 circles on the floor with water? Can the children label the fence posts using numerals by painting on them? Allow children to explore making a range of mathematical marks such as lines or tallies, shapes, numbers or patterns. Talk about the marks they have made and compare theirs with those of others. Can they use the correct language to describe the shapes or patterns they have created?

The water tray

Explain to the children that the water tray has got no equipment. What can they do to help? Involve the children in collecting resources such as bottles, jugs, cups, funnels, sieves, measuring spoons and buckets from home and the Early Years setting. Talk about how these items can be used in the water tray. Watch children as they play with the resources, noting the language they are using as they fill and pour. Can they draw conclusions linked to how much water each container will hold; which will hold the most/least? Demonstrate how to make marks on the containers to show how much water to pour into it. Let the children make their own marks and then fill the containers accordingly. Pose questions linked to how full the container is, how many spoons, for example, it takes to fill a cup or bottle, or if there is the correct amount of water in the container or too much/too little.

Water trays do not need to be overfilled with commercially made water toys, but should include some real and interesting objects such as shells and pebbles along with carefully chosen commercial resources such as nets, buckets and scoops.

Main activity 1

Skittles

You will need:

- Plastic bottles with a small amount of sand in the bottom of them
- Water pistols or squirty bottles
- Number cards
- Sticky labels
- Clipboards and paper

Getting started

Explain that the children are going to have a game of skittles but unfortunately there is no ball. All they have is water pistols or squirty bottles. How could they use these to knock down the skittles? Allow time for them to practise, for example against a wall.

Main activity

Set up the skittles with the children. Talk about getting points depending on the skittles that they knock down. How could they number them? Provide number cards or sticky labels for children to number the skittles. Arrange them with the largest numbered skittles at the back. Give each child a water pistol/squirty bottle. Explain that they have until the count of 10 to fire their water to see how many skittles they knock down. As children knock down the skittles encourage them to talk about the numbers on the skittles. How many did they knock down altogether? If they started with 10 skittles and knocked down 3, how many are still standing? Encourage them to record how many skittles they knocked down on their clipboard. Compare scores as more children play. Who knocked down the most/least? Extend this challenge to adding together the numbers of the skittles that they knock down; for example, if they knock down the 3 and the 4 they score 7 altogether. Use counting objects or fingers to find the correct answer. Who has scored the most? Is there another way of making the same total by knocking down different skittles? Again, ask children to record their scores and compare to find out who came 1st, 2nd, 3rd, etc. Make medals or certificates with the children. Can they find out who to give each medal to using their recordings?

What next?

- Pose questions for children to explore after undertaking the activity, such as what is the smallest number of squeezes or shots that it takes to knock down at least 3/5 skittles?

- If the children do not knock all their skittles down but have run out of water talk about how many times they think they will need to refill to knock down all the skittles. Test this and compare to their estimate.

- Repeat a similar game but instead of skittles create targets on the wall by chalking numbers on bricks. Who can use their bottles or water pistols to shoot each number? Can they shoot the numbers in order from 1–10, then to 20?

Main activity 2

Down the pipe

You will need:

- Large pipes or guttering
- Small world creatures (that are waterproof)
- A range of containers that hold different amounts of water such as jugs, cups, measuring spoons and bottles

Getting started

Link two water trays or large buckets using a large pipe or guttering. Explain that one of the small world creatures has got stuck in the pipe and can't get across to the other side. What can they do to help? Provide the children with a range of containers and talk about what they could do with these to solve the problem.

Main activity

Allow children time to negotiate with others regarding the choice of equipment to try and wash out the character. Help the children to fill one of the containers to an agreed point, such as 'half full'. Encourage the children to pour the water through the pipe or guttering and watch what happens. If the character is washed to the other tray/bucket talk about how much water they needed to wash it out. If not, encourage them to refill their container to continue to try and wash it

Adding water play to another type of provision can encourage children to apply and use their mathematical knowledge and skills. These children explored how quickly the water travelled down the slide and attempted to fill containers with the travelling water. The inclusion of real measuring jugs adds a real life and familiar element to the play.

through. Could the children mark on their container how much water they need to wash the character through? Compare the containers that each child uses. Do they need more spoons of water or cups? How many jugs did it take? Was this more or less than the small bottle? Can the children order the containers according to which took the most/fewest refills to wash the character through?

What next?

- Talk about how to measure how far the character travels once it has been washed out of the pipe/guttering. What equipment could they use to measure this? Which container makes the character travel the furthest?

- Make a simple table to record how many times each container is filled to wash the character through the pipe/guttering. Can the children use this table to find out which needed the most/fewest refills? Which container needed to be filled 3 times?

- Extend or shorten the length of the pipe/guttering. Can the children predict what will happen and the effect this will have on the amount of water needed to wash the character to the other side? Test their ideas and draw conclusions.

Look, listen and note

- What language are they using as they explore capacity, number, counting and shape?
- Do they talk about how full containers are as they fill or pour from them?
- How do children solve problems in the context of the water tray or outdoor area? Do they use their knowledge of capacity to inform their choices?
- Observe children's use of numbers, marks or tallies to record what they have found out.
- Do children sort objects or containers using their own criteria?

Key questions

- Can you tell me . . .?
- What do you notice when . . .?
- Can you order these containers by how much they hold?
- Can you match these containers to their shapes/to the objects?
- How full is your bucket/container?
- How could you record what you have done?

Key vocabulary

Counting: Number, zero, one, two, three up to ten, how many, how few

Calculating: More, and, altogether, one more, two more, leave, one less, two less, greatest, most, biggest, largest, least, fewest, smallest, add, plus, take (away)

Solving problems: Count, order, sort, same, different, match, find, choose, collect, use, make, tell me, describe, talk about, instructions, explain

Measures: Measure, size, compare, enough, not enough, too much, too little, too many, too few, nearly, close to, about the same as, full, half full, empty, holds, container

Shape: Side, flat, curved, straight, round, corner; (2D) circle, triangle, square, rectangle, star, oval

⊞ Health and safety

- Ensure children are supervised when using bubble mixture as this should not be put into the mouth or drunk.
- Ensure children are not using water for long periods of time in the outdoor area during very cold weather. Provide towels for children to be able to keep their hands dry after using water.
- Monitor the area around the water tray inside to ensure surfaces and floor areas are not wet or slippery.

📖 Useful stories and rhymes

5 little ducks (Traditional rhyme)
A well-known counting rhyme to introduce subtraction and one less.

Doctor Foster (Traditional rhyme)
A well-known nursery rhyme to promote the exploration of puddles.

Incy wincy spider (Traditional rhyme)
A favourite nursery rhyme which could be used as a starting point for 'Down the pipe'.

Noah's Ark (Bible story)
A religious story which can be used as an introduction to matching, sorting and counting in 2s.

Who Sank the Boat? (Pamela Allen, Picture Puffin, 1990)
A picture book that encourages talk about floating and sinking linked to the animals' weight in the boat.

Mr Archimedes' Bath (Pamela Allen, HarperCollins, 1993)
A story which can explore why water overflows when more and more of Mr Archimedes' friends get into the bath.

Links to theory

Jean Piaget

Children will have explored water since a very early age and will therefore have already created their own ideas about its properties and concepts such as capacity.

Piaget's work outlined stages that children progress through in their development. Between the ages 2 and 6 children are said to be working within the 'Pre-operational stage' during which they base their ideas on the immediate world around them and their experiences. Piaget stressed the importance of ensuring children have explored and therefore have developed an understanding of concepts before being taught knowledge or skills linked to larger concepts such as volume or capacity (Cooney, Cross & Trunk 1993).

What does this look like in practice?

Children need prolonged and frequent opportunities to play with and explore water in a range of contexts. It is important that they experience water in other parts of the setting than just merely a water tray. Children need to explore pouring water in a large outside area to find out what happens to water as it spreads and searches for a route downhill, using larger containers to fill and empty, and a range of equipment such as hoses and squeezy bottles. Before introducing difficult concepts such as ordering containers by their capacity, children need many opportunities to explore what happens when these containers are filled and emptied through play to form their own initial ideas.

Making mathematical marks

- Exploring different sized paint brushes on different surfaces
- Using water coloured with food colouring to make shapes and patterns
- Using squirty bottles or water pistols filled with water to make marks
- Making marks or records of what they have found out linked to capacity, sorting or scoring

2 | Sand

Why sand is important

This chapter will focus on the use of sand to develop children's early mathematical ideas in a range of exciting ways. Sand is a versatile resource which offers numerous opportunities for learning about pouring, filling, hiding and finding objects, talking about full and empty, sand timers and the properties of wet and dry sand. It can be used on a large and small scale offering kinaesthetic opportunities as children walk through the sand, feel it between their toes and make footprints. Their experience of sand in the wider world such as at the beach or at home in sand pits provides further opportunities to explore concepts developed within the setting.

Links to other areas of learning

Personal Social and Emotional Development	• Developing an awareness of the need for hygiene – washing their hands after using the sand • Selecting and using resources independently by choosing objects to hide and find in the sand • Working with others to undertake activities and share resources
Communication and Language	• Questioning why things happen and talking about their ideas • Negotiating plans with others and sharing their ideas when working inside or outside with sand

Literacy	• Writing their own stories or accounts about their trips to the beach or holidays they have been on • Stories and rhymes about the beach • Making marks in the sand, including letters, sounds and words • Hiding letters or words in the sand to find and record
Understanding the World	• Identifying similarities and differences between wet and dry sand • Talking about the changes that happen when water is added to sand linked to cause and effect • Using coloured sand to create rangoli patterns for Diwali • Investigating sand and hidden objects using all of their senses • Talking about past events in their life, for example previous trips they have made to the beach
Physical Development	• Handling a range of tools to move, pour, fill and dig safely • Using a range of equipment such as sieves, funnels, buckets and spades. • Keeping healthy by washing their hands after they have used sand
Expressive Arts and Design	• Using coloured sand to make pictures • Mixing sand with paint to create different textured effects and talking about how it changes the paint • Using sand to make musical instruments such as shakers • Developing an interest in the texture of sand when dry and wet, and how it feels when poured over their hands and feet • Singing songs about the beach and creating dance movements linked to creatures found at the seaside • Using seaside objects such as seaweed, stones, shells and driftwood to create 3D sculptures • Observational drawing of natural seaside objects, looking carefully at patterns, lines and shape
Mathematics	• Capacity • Weight • Counting • Number • Sorting • Calculating • Solving problems

Key resources

- A range of digging tools – spades, spoons, trowels
- Pouring and filling equipment – buckets, jugs, cups, bottles
- Funnels of varying sizes
- Sieves
- A range of counters, stones, sticks
- Numbers of varying sizes and materials
- Tubing
- Objects to hide in the sand – buttons, animals, pebbles
- Access to water nearby if possible

Maths web

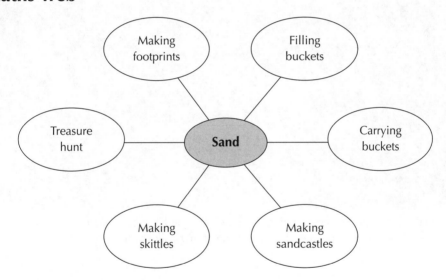

Filling buckets

Give the children a range of different-sized buckets and equipment to transport the sand. Talk to the children as they fill the buckets about how they could describe the amount of sand in each bucket, using language such as 'full', 'nearly full', 'nearly empty'. Discuss the different equipment the children could use to fill their buckets. How many spoons of sand will fill their bucket? Is that the same number of spoons that will fill their friend's or another sized bucket? What happens if they use cups instead of spoons to fill their buckets? Can they order the buckets by their capacity? How could they check if they are right? Talk to the children about how they could record how many spoons/cups of sand were needed to fill the bucket. Could they use drawings or make marks as labels to stick onto the bucket? Work with the children to create a large table to show how many spoons/cups of sand were needed, then compare to find out which needed the most/least. Encourage the children to ask each other questions about the capacity of the buckets after listening to those modelled by an adult.

It is vital to offer children opportunities to experience sand at different levels, sometimes on a table top, sometimes in a pit outside or in a builder's tray on the floor

Carrying buckets

Set the challenge to find out which is heavier to carry as a builder, buckets of dry or wet sand. Provide hats for children to become builders, a range of buckets and two trays of sand. Talk to the children about how to change the dry sand to wet sand. Let the children explore this, talking about pouring and filling buckets with water. How much water are they using? Is their bucket full, half full, nearly full of sand/water? What if they added 3 cups of water, what happens to the sand? 10 cups? Ask the children to think about how they will find out if wet or dry sand is heavier. Leave a range of different sized containers with the sand for the children to explore. Listen to the language they are using and talk to them about how they are solving the problem and what they have found out. Do they compare the buckets by holding one in each hand or do they use their own method?

Making sandcastles

Add a small amount of water to the sand. Give children a range of different-sized and -shaped buckets. Give children the opportunity to use a range of equipment to fill their buckets with sand. Talk to the children about how to check that their bucket is 'full'. As they are filling, encourage the use of language to talk about what they are doing, for example 'it is nearly full', 'it is half full'. Discuss whose bucket might hold the most/ least sand and how to check by looking at the resulting sandcastles. Turn the buckets over to make the sandcastles on the floor outside. Discuss the different sandcastles – are any the same? How are they different? How could they describe the size and shape of their sandcastles? Provide a range of measuring equipment such as tape measures, cubes and rulers and let children explore measuring the sandcastles to compare their heights.

Making skittles

Get a selection of empty water or drinks bottles and explain that you will be making a set of skittles for the outside area. Talk to the children about how much sand they think they will need to put in the skittles to make sure they stand up without falling over but can be knocked over with a soft ball. Try out their ideas to work out how full the bottles need to be. Discuss the most effective way to fill the bottles – what is the best piece of equipment to use to fill the bottle, for example a cup, spoon, jug? How many jugs would it take to fill the bottle to the right point? Do they think it would take more or less cups than jugs? How could they check? Once the skittles have been made, allow the children to number the skittles with their own mathematical marks. Use the skittles to play outside. What is the highest score they can get using one, or two balls? How could they record their scores? Provide clipboards and large whiteboards to encourage children to record their scores. Model writing number sentences to show the total of the scores from the skittles.

Treasure hunt

Hide a selection of counters, cubes, shells or stones in the sand. Explain that a pirate has buried his treasure but can't remember how much treasure he has got. How can the children help? Allow children time to explore digging for treasure using spades or spoons and collect their treasure in their buckets. How could they work out how many pieces of treasure they have collected? Explore with children different ways to count their treasure, for example by touching each as they count, laying them out on the floor in a line and counting them, and then looking at the treasure in different arrangements to check if they still have the same number if they are moved. Provide stickers or small pieces of paper for children to record how many pieces of treasure they have found.

Making footprints

Have a large tray with a layer of sand mixed with a little water. Ask a range of children to remove their shoes and make footprints in the sand. Talk about the similarities and differences between the footprints. How many footprints can they count? How many toes can they see? Count the toes in fives as you touch each footprint, or in tens as you touch each pair of feet. Discuss how to find out who has the biggest feet. What will they need to do? What could they use to measure the footprints? Allow time for the children to explore measuring the footprints in different ways. Discuss their findings. Can they match the footprints to the person who made them?

 ### Main activity 1

Decorating sandcastles
You will need:

- Pictures of sandcastles
- Natural and commercially prepared resources for decorating
- 1st, 2nd and 3rd prize flags
- Ready-made sandcastles (as part of 'Making sandcastles' activity)

Getting started

Explain that you are hosting a sandcastle competition in which they are going to take part with the sandcastles they made as part of the 'Making sandcastles' activity. Talk about the resources that they could use to decorate the sandcastles. Show children a range of large pictures of sandcastles of different sizes and shapes. Talk about the similarities and differences between the sandcastles and then look at the sandcastles the children have made. Are any of their sandcastles similar to the ones in the pictures? What differences can they see?

Main activity

Explain that children will need to plan their sandcastle before decorating to ensure it looks as interesting as possible. Provide children with the large sandcastle pictures for them to plan how to decorate their sandcastle with natural/

commercially prepared resources. Can they record on the plan how many of each resource they will need? Allow children to collect the correct number of resources that they have chosen on the plan. While the children are decorating their sandcastle talk about the choices they are making, for example how many stones will they use? How tall will their flags be? How will they check their flags are the same height? How many stones and flags do they have altogether? Compare the sandcastles for a sandcastle competition. Count the number of decorations used and compare to the plans. Award 1st, 2nd and 3rd prizes to the sandcastles – ask the children to make award badges for the winning sandcastles.

What next?

- Give prepared lists of resources for children to follow such as 4 stones, 5 twigs or 3 buttons to decorate sandcastles. Can they check each other's sandcastles to ensure they have the correct number of each resource?

- Challenge the children to only being allowed 10 (or any given number) of resources altogether. Who can make their sandcastle look the most interesting with this number of resources? How can we check that they have used the right number of resources altogether? What if they had 1/2 more, how many would they have then?

- Explain that they now have two sandcastles to decorate and a given number of resources (such as 5, 10, 20). How many will they put on each of the sandcastles? How can they check that they have used the correct number altogether? How many different ways can they decorate the two sandcastles using those resources? What if there were three sandcastles to decorate?

Main activity 2

Here comes the sea

You will need:

- Sandcastles (made in 'Making sandcastles' activity)
- Buckets of varying sizes and shapes
- Water
- Clipboards with paper
- Number cards
- Pencils or chalks

Getting started

After the children have made their sandcastles talk about what happens at the beach to sandcastles in the sand. This could be linked to a story or song about sandcastles falling down or being washed away. How much water do they think it might take to wash the sandcastles away? Children to make predictions (based on small buckets of water). How could these predictions be recorded? Look at recording names with marks/tallies/numerals or children having the number of counters to represent their predictions to remember their guess. These could be recorded on paper or drawn using chalk on the floor of the outdoor area.

Main activity

Talk about how to fill the bucket and whether it should be full, half full or nearly full of water each time to check that it is fair. Let the children fill the bucket to half full, nearly full and full to make a decision. Can they all fill the bucket to make it full? Provide a range of different-sized buckets. Talk about which should be used to test the sandcastles. What do they think would happen if they used a bigger/smaller bucket? Allow children time to explore how many full buckets it takes to wash the sandcastles away. Is the same number of buckets needed for all the sandcastles or do some take more/less? How could they record what they have found out? Explore the idea of drawing sandcastles and recording the number of buckets of water to wash them away using number cards, numerals or marks. Compare these findings with predictions. Did anyone guess the same number? Is the result more or less than our prediction? How many more/less? Repeat the investigation using bigger and smaller buckets. What happens if a smaller bucket is used? How can we record this?

What next?

- After finding out how many buckets of water it takes to wash one sandcastle away can the children predict and then find out how many buckets it would take to wash two of the same-sized sandcastles away?
- Instead of filling the buckets to the top can they find out how many times they would need to use the buckets if they were only half full?
- Children to take photos of their investigation and then make their own mathematical labels to show how many buckets it took to wash the sandcastles away for display.

Look, listen and note

- What language do the children use to describe capacity of weight, for example heavier, lighter, full, half full, empty, nearly full?
- What methods are the children using to solve a problem, such as how many more or fewer buckets they need compared to their predictions?
- How do the children count their resources? Do they show 1 to 1 correspondence? Do they know that the number of objects does not change even if the set is moved?
- How do children choose to record their findings? Do they use tallies, marks or numerals? Do they record their ideas through drawings?

Key questions

- How many . . . can you count?
- How do you know that you have counted them all?
- Can you tell me how full your bucket is of water/sand?
- What would happen if you used a smaller/bigger bucket?
- Can you guess how many you will need? Were you right?

Key vocabulary

Counting: Number: zero, one, two, three up to ten, how many; count: many, few, guess how many, estimate, first, second, third up to tenth

Calculating: Add, more, and, make, total, altogether, one more, two more, take (away), one less, two less, is the same as

Solving problems: Sort, order, same, different, find, choose, collect, use, make, tell me, describe, talk about, explain, draw, record, tell me, same, different

Measures: Measure, size, compare, enough, not enough, too much, too little, too many, too few, nearly, full, half full, empty, holds, container, length, height, long, short, tall, high, low, weighs, balances, heavy/light, heavier/lighter, heaviest/lightest, balance, scales

⊞ Health and safety

- Ensure children are supervised when using sand to avoid accidents when digging, for example getting sand in their eyes.
- Children need to be reminded not to put objects into their mouths and adults need to be vigilant when children are using small items.
- Adults need to ensure sand is clear of sharp objects before children put their hands or feet into it.

📖 Useful stories and rhymes

The wise man and the foolish man (Bible story)
A good starting point for introducing wet and dry sand.

She sells sea shells on the sea shore, the shells she sells are surely sea shells (Traditional rhyme)
This tongue twister links to the treasure hunt activity, discussing the natural treasures of the seashore.

Lucy and Tom at the Seaside (Shirley Hughes, Picture Puffin, 1993)
A good starting point for discussion about children's experience of the beach, building sandcastles and watching the tide.

Come Away from the Water Shirley (John Burningham, Red Fox, 1992)
Supports the development of the imagination as children join Shirley looking for buried treasure (link to treasure activities).

Sandcastle (Kipper) (Mick Inkpen, Hodder Children's Books, 1998)
A story about the challenges of making sandcastles (a lovely starting point for sandcastle activities).

▨ Links to theory

John Comenius

The importance of sand was highlighted by Comenius who believed that sensory experiences are at the heart of education rather than learning by rote. These beliefs helped to shape future developments in education, particularly regarding our views on how children learn as he believed children learn through play (Pound 2005). It is evident how this has impacted on current practice, as sensory experiences, such as sand and water, are central elements of continuous provision in all Early Years settings.

What does this look like in practice?

Sand should be available for children to use daily within settings, both inside and outdoors. Through play and the careful choice of equipment, children can develop their own ideas, such as what happens when a bucket has holes in the bottom, or when sand is poured from a height. The use of a sand tray is valuable to develop collaborative learning; however sand should also be experienced in other containers for children to gain a real understanding of its properties. Activities such as pouring sand using large equipment, moving or carrying it in a variety of containers or touching and standing in it with bare feet to feel the sand between fingers and toes can all be key experiences for young children.

Making mathematical marks

- Using twigs and sticks to make marks in the sand
- Keeping tallies for games or recording scores using marks
- Beginning to record number sentences for games on clipboards or whiteboards
- Finding ways to record sorting activities using paper or chalks in the outside area
- Using hands, fingers and feet to make marks in the sand
- Finding ways to record the sandcastles they make before they wash away (on paper, with a camera, etc.) and using these to build again another day

3 | Dough

Why dough is important

This chapter explores the potential of dough to develop children's early mathematical ideas and thinking. This is an exciting material because children learn both through using and exploring the dough and through the actual process of making it. These experiences offer a wealth of rich learning opportunities relating to measures, materials and changes. It is vital that young children have the opportunity to work with large amounts of dough, not just small tubs (such as those bought commercially). Dough is cheap and simple to make. It can easily be changed through the use of colourings, spices, flavourings or other material such as glitter and sequins.

Links to other areas of learning

Personal Social and Emotional Development	• Sharing equipment, taking turns and working alongside each other
	• Developing a sense of ownership when children are involved in making the dough themselves and making choices about what to add
	• Offering an outlet for emotional release as children can express anger or frustration as they manipulate dough; it also provides a calming therapeutic experience as children knead and explore it, especially when it's warm and freshly made

Communication and Language	• Developing descriptive language to describe the textures, appearance and smells of the dough, which can be easily adapted • Promoting social talk as children engage in dough play and naturally chat to each other
Literacy	• Using long sausage shapes to form familiar letters, reinforcing correct letter formation • Supporting pre writing skills as children pinch, pull and use various tools such as tweezers, rollers and cutters • Developing reading skills as children follow simple recipes to make their dough
Understanding the World	• Offering opportunities for learning about and exploring mixtures • Providing first-hand experiences of change and materials as the dough is made and becomes a solid mass • Exploring dough using the senses of touch, sight and smell
Physical Development	• Offering opportunities for children to develop both large-scale and small-scale movements • Providing opportunities to pinch, pull, twist and stretch
Expressive Arts and Design	• Developing the imagination as children make models using the dough • Allowing children to explore colours as coloured doughs are mixed together • Using dough to make props for role play such as food or to support songs and rhymes such as currant buns and fat sausages
Mathematics	• Measuring (including time) • Shape and space • Number • Counting • Pattern • Calculating

Key resources

- Dough (and ingredients, see recipes)
- Tweezers, chopsticks, pizza cutters and other tools
- Small objects such as buttons, sequins, pasta shapes (uncooked)
- Rolling pins
- Bun trays
- Silicone or paper cake cases
- Chocolate box inserts
- Shaker pots of glitter, and spices such as cinnamon or mixed spice
- Colouring and flavourings

Maths web

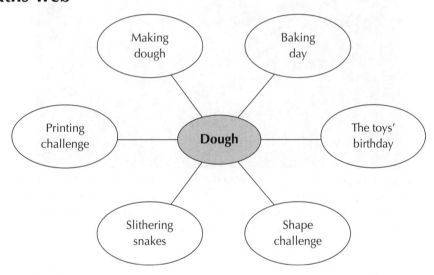

Baking day

Provide the children with a range of empty chocolate box inserts, cake trays and bun cases. Also offer chef hats, dough, candles and other small objects to decorate the cakes such as buttons, glass pebbles and shells. Turn a cardboard box into a pretend oven and provide a range of timers for the children to explore such as sand timers, digital timers, stopwatches and cooking timers. Children will enjoy making their cakes, filling the cases and decorating them with the small objects. This can lead to discussions about different types of cakes, birthdays and celebrations, and waiting 1, 2, 5 or 10 minutes for things to cook.

The dough area does not need to be filled with commercial brightly coloured cutters. Empty containers from home are cheap and easy to find and add a real-life dimension to play. The use of hands as primary tools not only develops fine motor skills but enables children to learn about quantities in a sensory way.

The toys' birthday

Collect some soft toys and birthday badges showing different ages. Attach the badges to the soft toys. Explain to the children that the toys are all celebrating their birthdays. Can the children tell how old the toys are? Who is the oldest? Youngest? Same age as them/ their brother/sister? Children love the excitement of big numbers so perhaps add an adult-age badge into the equation! Tell the children that the toys are very upset because no one has made them any birthday cakes. What could the children do to help? Provide dough, cake tins, cake cases, chef hats and cut-up straws to be candles. Older children could cut up their own straws and try to ensure that their 'candles' are the same length. Talk to the children about how many candles they think they will need and whether an older toy will need a bigger cake. Once the children have made their cakes, challenge them to match the right cakes to the right toys. Who had the most/fewest candles? How old will they be next year?

Shape challenge

Provide some pictures of common 2D shapes, for example circle, square, triangle, rectangle (or plastic 2D shapes) and explain to the children that you couldn't find the shape cutters anywhere to use with the dough. Look at the pictures/shapes with the children and talk about them using everyday language: straight, round, long, short, corners, etc. Challenge them to try to make some shapes from their dough using various tools: lollipop sticks, scissors, plastic knives, pizza cutters. Talk to them about the shapes they are making and their properties. How many sides will a shape have? Will they be straight or curved? Once the children have made their shapes talk about how they are the same and different from others in the group. Can their friends see which ones they have made? Can they sort their shapes and match them with others their friends have made?

Slithering snakes

Take some time to show the children how to roll snakes. Give each child a small ball of dough and encourage them all to have a go at making their own snakes. Challenge them to make the snakes as long as they can without breaking. Once everyone has made a snake compare them and talk about which one is longest, shortest, skinniest, fattest and so on. Ask the children if they can draw around their snakes on some paper. These could be cut out for a display. Tell the children you would like to make a snake to go all the way along the table/across the floor and suggest putting all the snakes together in a long line. Model how to join them by pinching the dough together. How far can the snake reach now? This could be moved onto some wallpaper for the children to draw around. Can they fit all the snakes they drew earlier underneath it?

Printing challenge

Gather together a range of small objects that would make good imprints on the dough such as shells, buttons, coins, plastic construction bricks and cotton reels. Start by encouraging the children to roll their dough flat on the table. Explain that they are going to try making some patterns using the objects. Talk about the prints they think they will make. Once the children have explored this, put the children into pairs and blindfold one child whilst the other chooses an object to print with and does this on their dough. Their partner removes their blindfold and has to guess which object was used. This can be extended to copying linear patterns underneath and talking about repeating patterns.What would come next? Can they use two objects to make a repeating pattern? Or three?

Making dough

Prepare a simple pictorial recipe to show the children, illustrating the number of cups/spoons of each ingredient needed. Take photos of the children as they mix the dough to make a photographic recipe for them to use in the future to make their own dough or whilst playing. If you choose to make the uncooked dough children can have their own individual portions and can freely choose which colours, flavourings or textures they would like to add. A cooked version requires an agreement on these issues, perhaps by a vote which could be supported by some early mathematical mark making to show preferences (smiley faces, tallies, ticks, crosses). How many people want pink, green, blue, yellow dough? Encourage the children to measure out the ingredients and help count the number of cups/spoons added. This activity provides numerous opportunities to use ordinal language (first, second, third) and language of time such as next, then, after, finally and so on. Once the dough is made, children need time to explore the dough freely. Warm, freshly made dough offers a therapeutic sensory experience. Even when dough goes wrong and becomes sticky or too sloppy this can provide excellent learning opportunities to problem solve and find ways to make it right and consider the importance of measuring correctly!

Main activity 1

Salt dough numbers
You will need:

- Numbers written on A4 card and laminated (1–5 or 10)
- Salt dough (see recipe)
- Paint

Getting started

Prepare some large numerals on A4 card either hand written or using the computer, and laminate these. Make some salt dough with the children using the recipes provided. Explain to the children that you need them to make some numbers to help everyone in the setting/class practise their counting and learn their numbers.

Main activity

Begin by showing the children how to make long sausage shapes and encourage them to do the same. Once everyone has made a long sausage shape, ask each child to choose a number card. Do the children know which number it is? Can they see it anywhere in the setting? Where have they seen this number before? Encourage them to look at the shapes of the numbers and discuss this together using everyday language: straight, curly, curved, down, up and so on. Encourage the children to think about what animals or objects the numbers might look like; for example, number two could be a swan with a long neck or number one like a lamp post. Ask the children to put their sausages on top of the number cards to form the numerals, offering lots of opportunities for them to trace the shape with their finger over the dough and in the air, talking about the shape and direction taken to form the number. Explain that the numbers are going to be cooked and talk about the temperature dial. Show the children a range of timers and tell them that they can choose which one to use. Think about how the numbers look different (i.e. digital and analogue). Cook the numbers, asking the children to listen out for the timer. Once the numbers have cooled, the children can paint them. They could choose to use one colour or to make patterns such as spots, stripes, wavy lines and so on.

What next?

- Use the children's salt dough numbers in interactive displays, for play activities, and as a visual prop when reciting number rhymes, counting songs and stories.

- Provide a range of mark making materials such as chalks, pens, pencils and crayons and use the dough numbers as templates for children to draw around to reinforce number recognition and correct formation.

- Hide the numerals around the setting (inside and out) and challenge children to find them. Can they record which numbers they find on their clipboards? Who found the most numbers? What were the biggest and smallest numbers they found? Children could also take photos of the numbers and use these to make a number line.

Main activity 2

Pizza time!

You will need:

- A large amount of uncoloured plain dough
- Chef hats and aprons

- Rolling pins and pizza cutters
- Bowls of dried pasta, buttons, cut-up drinking straws, plastic counters
- Dice with 1,1,2,2,3,3 spots or numerals.

Getting started

Some pizza restaurant chains happily accept groups for visits and this could be a great opportunity for children to learn about the pizza restaurant environment.

Begin by giving each child a ball of dough and explaining that today you are all working in a busy pizza restaurant. Talk about who has eaten pizza before and the sort of things that go onto it. Ask the children about the base of a pizza. Do the children know what the base is made of? Do they prefer a thick or a thin base? What shape bases have they seen? Challenge them to make their own pizza base in any thickness or shape they like from the dough, but explain that they will need to have lots of room for toppings! Once they have all prepared their base, look at them and encourage the children to think about the different shapes, sizes and thicknesses.

Main activity

Talk to the children about the various toppings they might have on their pizza. Which ones have they had before? Which ones are their favourite? Which ones don't they like? Show the children 4 separate bowls of buttons, pasta pieces, cut up drinking straws and plastic counters and tell them that these are their pizza toppings. Can they think of what these could be? For example, the buttons could be tomatoes, the counters could be mushrooms. Encourage them to share their own ideas. Show the children the 1–3 spotted/numbered dice. Explain that the dice will tell them how many toppings they need for their pizza. Each child rolls the dice and is free to choose any of the toppings for the pizza. After each child has rolled the dice several times, look at the pizzas that have been made. Which one has the most/fewest toppings?

What next?

- Children could attempt to record their pizzas by drawing them, taking photos of them or making a lists of what is on them using their own mathematical marks to record the number of each topping.

- Play could be developed by cooking the pizzas in a _pretend_ oven, talking about temperature and timing (you could provide a range of timers for children to explore).
- Children could also use pizza cutters to slice their pizzas and find out how many people could eat a slice each. How big would a pizza need to be for everyone to have a slice?

Look, listen and note

- Do children enjoy counting activities and use number names correctly? Are they beginning to recognise any numerals, including those of personal importance?
- Are they able to match shapes and patterns and talk about these using everyday familiar language?
- Do they talk about the size of their dough using language such as big, small, fat, thin, etc?
- Are they using their developing ideas to solve problems in practical contexts?

? Key questions

- What do you think you might need to do here?
- Can you tell me about the shape/pattern you have made?
- What are you going to try next?
- I wonder what would happen if . . .?
- Can you tell me about what you have been doing?

Key vocabulary

Counting: Count, guess how many, 1, 2, 3 up to 10, more, less, same, different

Measures: Big, biggest, small, smallest, fat, fattest, thin, thinnest, long, longest, short, shortest

Shape: Circle, round, rectangle, corner, sides, square, triangle, pointy, straight, curved

Time: Measure, how long, time, minute, temperature, timer, clock

Solving problems: Decide, choose, share, half, how many, altogether

Pattern: Pattern, repeating pattern, match

Health and safety

- Be aware of any allergies to ensure the ingredients (especially colourings and food stuffs) in your dough do not pose any problems.
- Children need to be reminded not to put dough or other objects into their mouths, especially as the dough contains a large amount of salt. Adults need to be vigilant with regard to this.
- Cooked dough will keep for a couple of weeks in an airtight container, but should ideally be replaced regularly to ensure good hygiene. Other types of dough may only last a day.
- Only adults should use the oven when cooking salt dough. Hot trays and utensils must be kept out of reach of the children. Adults need to remind children to stay away from the oven and also ensure that the area is supervised and zoned off.

Useful stories and rhymes

Pat a cake, pat a cake (Traditional rhyme)

This is the way we knead our dough/ cut our dough/ pinch our dough/ roll our dough/ squash our dough (to the tune of 'Here we go round the mulberry bush') (Traditional rhyme)
Both of these rhymes could be sung/recited as children work with the dough.

The Little Red Hen (Traditional tale)
This story offers opportunities for children to explore adding and mixing ingredients together and sharing amounts.

Jack and Me and the Pizza (Early Worms, Franklin Watts Limited, 1997)
Introduces numbers one to ten linked to pizzas.

Links to theory

Jean-Jacques Rousseau

Rousseau was probably one of the earliest advocators of a child-centred approach to education. He proposed that in their early years children should be learning by doing, through practical and physical experiences linked to their interests and abilities. Rousseau strongly believed that children need to develop their physical skills and senses (Sutherland 1988). This demonstrates the importance of the dough area in the Early Years setting.

What does this look like in practice?

In any Early Years setting it is vital that children have regular opportunities to develop their senses and physical skills through accessing stimulating and interesting resources. Dough is an example of such a resource as it can easily be enhanced to stimulate the senses through the addition of colours, scents and textures. Its very texture calls for it to be kneaded, twisted, rolled, stretched and pulled. Dough is a resource that children are able to access at their own physical level, whether merely squashing and squeezing it or using it to make models.

Making mathematical marks

- Encourage children to use different tools to make marks in their dough.
- Children can make their own price labels for dough cakes they make or try to record marks to indicate the number of candles on cakes.
- Practise number formation on a large scale in the air, using sausages from dough, on whiteboards and clipboards and talking about the shapes and direction taken.
- Record pizzas and making lists of ingredients.
- Make birthday cards, badges, banners and flags for the soft toys' birthdays using their own marks to indicate numbers and amounts.

Dough recipes

Classic dough

- 3 cups of plain flour
- 3 cups of water
- Food colouring/flavourings as required
- 1½ cups of salt
- 3 tablespoons of cooking oil
- 6 teaspoons of cream of tartar

Put all ingredients together into a saucepan and stir continuously over a medium heat. After a while the mixture will start to thicken and become difficult to stir. Heat until the mixture forms a dough and you are happy with the consistency.

This dough keeps well in an airtight container.

Salt dough

- 4 cups of flour
- 1 cup of salt
- 1½ cups of water

Mix the ingredients together well and then knead into a ball, adding a little extra water if the dough will not hold together. Make sure any surface where you are planning to use the dough is lightly floured to prevent sticking. Bake items on a tray for about an hour at 180°C; thinner items will cook more quickly and may need to be removed sooner to prevent burning. Once cooled, items can be painted with normal paint and when dry coated with a PVA glue and water mixture to varnish.

4 | **Construction**

Why construction is important

This chapter will focus on the use of construction to develop children's early mathematical ideas in a range of exciting ways. This is often a busy area in Early years settings which naturally encourages children to explore 3D shape, position, direction, colour, size, height and counting as they build and construct. Children can work on large or small scales with a whole range of resources including commercially bought bricks or even empty cardboard boxes, both inside and outside. This area of provision is particularly popular with boys and therefore a wonderful opportunity to encourage reluctant writers to record mathematical ideas and the use of rich mathematical vocabulary.

Links to other areas of learning

Personal Social and Emotional Development	• Selecting and using resources independently by choosing the type of construction equipment to use or junk resources to complete their structures
	• Working with others to plan and undertake construction, developing cooperation and team work to complete large-scale projects
	• Developing concentration by completing ongoing construction projects over sustained periods of time
	• Team challenges such as 'What is the tallest structure you can build using newspaper?' (ensure groups work together to plan and undertake the activity)

Communication and Language	<ul><li>Questioning why things happen, for example why tall structures often fall over</li><li>Talking about their ideas and choices during planning and evaluating structures</li><li>Negotiating plans with others to complete a project successfully</li></ul>
Literacy	<ul><li>Making marks to label structures or plans/designs</li><li>Stories and rhymes about building</li><li>Reading non-fiction books about buildings and structures</li></ul>
Understanding the World	<ul><li>Identifying similarities and differences between materials and structures</li><li>Talking about the changes that happen; for example, what happens to concrete when it dries</li><li>Investigating structures and materials using all of their senses</li><li>Talking about key buildings in their past/current lives such as hospitals, churches, houses</li><li>Looking at different structures from a variety of countries and cultures and comparing them with familiar buildings in their local area</li></ul>
Physical Development	<ul><li>Handling a range of tools to construct safely such as scissors, stapler, hole punch, tape</li><li>Developing large-scale motor control by handling construction equipment and moving, placing and arranging structures</li></ul>
Expressive Arts and Design	<ul><li>Using paint to decorate structures made from junk modelling materials</li><li>Singing songs about building and creating movements linked to the process of building such as mixing, climbing ladders, spreading and carrying materials</li><li>Creating pieces of music based on building by using building materials to make a variety of sounds, for example hammering noises, bricks clinking together or rattling screws in pots</li><li>Looking at patterns and colour in buildings and structures in the local area</li><li>Using different junk material to make different sounds, such as blowing through tubes, drumming with boxes</li><li>Planning projects orally or completing simple plans to show what they intend to construct</li></ul>

Mathematics	
	• Height
	• Length
	• Shape
	• Number
	• Counting
	• Calculating

Key resources

- A range of bricks – real and pretend of different shapes and sizes
- Wooden/plastic/foam blocks
- Buckets, wheelbarrows
- Plastic poles/sticks
- Fabric in a range of different colours and sizes
- Junk modelling resources such as large and small boxes, tubes and pots
- A variety of plastic and real building tools – hammers, screwdrivers, spanners, saws
- Safety equipment – hard hats, gloves, high visibility jackets, goggles
- Real and pretend nails and screws

Maths web

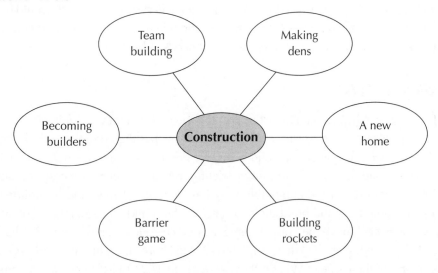

Making dens

Give children a range of different-sized plastic poles or strong sticks of varying lengths and a variety of different-sized and -shaped fabric. Leave this equipment in an open space for children to explore den making. Talk to them about how they are planning to build their den. Children could be given clipboards to record what they would like their den to look like. Observe which sticks/poles they use, talk about decisions, such as which would they choose to make the tallest/smallest den? Which would be best to match the pole/stick they have already chosen? What will happen if one pole/stick is longer/shorter than the other? What is the best shape to arrange the poles/sticks if they have 3? 4? What happens if the sticks are all close together? What if they were far apart? Once the den is made, evaluate it using the original plan. Is it the same or are there any differences? Who is the tallest person that could stand in the den? How many children could they fit inside the den?

A new home

Show the children three toys/puppets that have no home. Talk to them about what they could use to build the toys/puppets a new home. Encourage children to access their own resources. Explain that the house has to be the right size for each toy/puppet. How will they know how tall to build their structure? How could they measure each puppet/toy to inform their plans? Provide paper strips, tape measures, rulers, towers of cubes or bricks to help the children measure the height of the toys/puppets. Allow children time to build their structures. Once they are built reflect on whether the structures are the correct size. Measure the houses using the measuring equipment and compare the size and height of each of the homes that have been built. Which is the tallest/shortest? Which would be the best for the middle-sized toy? Smallest toy? Test the homes using the toys and talk about alterations that may need to be made, such as 'it needs to be taller'.

Building rockets

Using a story or toy spaceman as a stimulus, tell the children they are going to have the opportunity to build a rocket to visit space. Explain that they are allowed to choose 8/10/15 pieces of equipment to build a rocket. Provide a range of resources such as large boxes, building blocks and junk modelling resources such as tubes. Talk about the shapes and sizes of the equipment they have chosen. Allow time for children to select their equipment and build their rockets. Gather children together to look at the rockets – does each have the correct number of pieces? How can we check? What if a rocket has more/fewer than it should have? Are there any similarities/differences between any of the rockets? What if they were given 1/2/3 more pieces of equipment. How many would they have? Would the new rocket be taller/shorter than the first one?

It is essential that children have access to real-life mathematical tools to help solve their own real-life problems.

Discuss how to record what they have done through drawings, mark making or photographs. They could take their own photographs and then create captions for these linked to the number of items they have used for their rockets.

Barrier game

Children to sit facing each other with a barrier between them and the same construction equipment, such as two sets of identical building blocks of varying colours. One child builds a structure using the blocks behind the barrier. This child then describes to the other child (who cannot see the structure) how to build it, using positional language.

The other child follows the instructions to build the structure. The barrier is then removed and the structures are compared. Are they the same? What are the differences? How can they be made to look identical? Children will then swap over and the other child builds the structure. Ask the children to think about how they could record the structures they have created. Can they record the numbers of blocks used? How will they show the position of them? Could they write instructions for someone else to build their structures after talking through the sequence of building with a partner or adult?

Becoming builders

Talk about the job of builder. What do builders do? What do they use? Explain that builders often needs to move bricks from one place to another when they are building. Provide a range of buckets and wheelbarrows and real/play bricks. Talk to the children about how they could move the bricks from one side of the outdoor area to the other. Which bucket or wheelbarrow do they think will hold the most bricks? How could they find out? Allow children to try out their ideas and observe how they solve the problem. Support their ideas by suggesting counting the number of bricks that will make the bucket or wheelbarrow full. Compare each and ask the children to decide which holds the most. Now challenge the children to work out how many trips it would take to carry all of the bricks from one place to another. Can they guess? How could they find out? What if they used a different bucket or wheelbarrow. Would it mean more or fewer trips? Compare results. How could they record their findings?

Play with uniformly sized and shaped blocks encourages children to problem solve and explore shape and space purposefully.

Team building

Explain to the children that they will be developing their ability to work as a team to construct. Allow them to decide as a team the type of resources they want to use, for example small plastic bricks or large cardboard boxes. Provide the children with a range of dice (spotted and numbered in a range of sizes). Children take turns to use the dice to show how many building items they will take on their turn to create a structure. As each child has a go at rolling the dice they may take that number of bricks/boxes to add to the structure, negotiating with others about where to put them, for example 'on top', 'next to the tower', 'behind the house'. Watch the children and note the language they are using when negotiating. Pose questions such as 'How many do you have altogether now?' 'What if someone rolls a 2, how many will you have then?'

Main activity 1

Construction competition

You will need:

- Wooden/plastic/foam bricks
- One-minute sand timer
- Tape measure
- String
- Paper strips
- Metre stick
- Stickers/paper

Getting started

Show the children a box of wooden/plastic/foam bricks. Explain that these are the only bricks they can use for their building. If there are 2 or 4 children building today, how will they work out how many they can have each? Can they guess how many they think they could have each? Check by sharing out the bricks.

Main activity

Tell the children that there is a challenge to see who can make the longest/tallest structure using their bricks in one minute. Show the children the sand timer and demonstrate how it works. Allow time for children to think and plan their ideas before beginning. Encourage them to talk about how they are going to solve the problem. Children undertake the challenge. Can they talk about what they have done to build their structure (encouraging the use of positional language)? Afterwards talk about what each child has done. Which is the tallest/longest? How do we know? Show the children a range of measuring equipment such as tape measures, string, paper strips and a metre stick. Ask the children to talk about how they would find out which is the tallest/longest. Allow the children time to explore their ideas. Which is the best way? How could we put the towers in order of height/length if we did not have any measuring equipment? Work together to order the structures by height or length. Children to award prize stickers for the structures that have received 1st, 2nd, 3rd.

What next?

- Pose questions for children to explore after undertaking the activity, such as can you make a structure that is shorter than the structure that came 3rd ? Can you make a taller/longer structure than the one that came 1st/2nd?

- Provide children with a range of different construction equipment such as boxes, bricks, small coloured plastic bricks and explain that they will now set up their own challenge. Who can build the tallest tower in one minute? What about 5 minutes? 10 seconds?

- Give the children the 1st, 2nd and 3rd prize stickers. Encourage children to find 3 objects from within the setting or in the outdoor area and award them prizes (1st for the longest, 3rd for the shortest). Can they then make their own prize stickers up to 5th place? Can they find objects to match to 1st, 2nd, 3rd, 4th and 5th?

Main activity 2

Fallen bridges
You will need:

- Blue fabric or a drape
- A range of boxes
- Blocks or bricks of different 3D shapes
- Paper
- Pens/chalks

Getting started

Use a story or rhyme linked to bridges falling down as a starting point. Then show children a blue piece of fabric or a drape with boxes/blocks/bricks of different 3D shapes on the fabric. Explain that the bridge has fallen down and you don't know how to put it back together again.

Main activity

Allow children to talk together about their plan for how to rebuild the bridge. Talk to the children about the different-shaped resources. Which will be the best for the base of the bridge? Would a cone, sphere or curved shape be a good choice? How can they describe the shapes they have chosen? How are the shapes different? If the bridge is going to have a flat top what shapes could they use? Which items have flat faces? As the children build, discuss the choices of shapes, how they will ensure the sides of the bridge are the same height and how to find a shape that will reach between the two sides to create the top of the bridge. Once completed evaluate the bridge. Could any smaller shapes be used to decorate the top of the bridge? How many of the shapes can they name? Ask the children for ideas about how to record what they have done. Support children in creating a simple table with pictures of each shape in one column and the children can then count how many of each they have used and record them using marks in the other column. Which shape did they use the most/least? What if they were given 3 more shapes, what would they choose and where would they put them?

What next?

- Give children the same resources but this time explain that, instead of a bridge, a house has fallen down. Can they rebuild it? How could they record how many of each shape they have used this time for their structure?

- Give children a ready-made table completed with the number of each 3D shape for the structure. Can they use the table to select the right number of each shape? Can they then use these shapes to make their own structure? Has anyone made a different structure using the same shapes?

- Give children some pictures of structures such as castles, houses, bridges made out of 3D shapes. Can the children use these as a guide to copy and create these structures? Have they used the correct shapes in the correct positions? Can they talk about the structure they have made and shapes they have used? Take photos of their own structures for their friends to copy.

Look, listen and note

- What language are they using as they explore shape, measures, size and counting?
- How do they share objects, ensuring all children have an equal amount?
- How do children match shapes by identifying similarities and are they able to choose a named shape for a particular purpose?
- Consider children's use of positional language.
- Are they using their developing ideas to solve problems in the context?
- How do they record their findings – using sorting, numbers, pictures or marks?

? Key questions

- How can you describe the structures that you have built?
- What shapes can you notice?
- Are the structures the same or are they different? How could you describe them?
- What could you try next?
- How can you find out how many bricks/boxes you have used?
- What would happen if . . .?

Key vocabulary

Counting: Number, zero, one, two, three up to ten, how many, guess how many, estimate, nearly, first, second, third up to tenth

Calculating: More, altogether, one more, leave, one less

Solving problems: Count, order, sort, same, different, find, choose, collect, use, make, build, tell me, describe, instructions, explain

Measures: Measure, size, compare, enough, not enough, length, height, long, short, tall, full, half full, empty, holds, container

Shape: Face, side, edge, end, flat, curved, straight, round, hollow, solid, corner; (3D) cube, pyramid, sphere, cone; (2D) circle, triangle, square, rectangle, star, oval

Position: Over, under, above, below, top, bottom, side, on, in, in front, behind

⊕ Health and safety

- Ensure children are supervised when using large-scale building resources, especially when using heavy or sharp building equipment.
- Ensure children have appropriate protective clothing such as gloves when handling real building equipment and resources, such as bricks.

📖 Useful stories and rhymes

Humpty Dumpty (Traditional rhyme)
A well-known nursery rhyme to introduce building walls and structures.

This is the house that Jack built (Traditional rhyme)
A repetitive rhyme that can be used as a starting point for building houses or homes, for example 'A new home' or 'Becoming builders'.

London Bridge is falling down (Traditional rhyme)
A traditional song which could be a lovely starting point for 'Fallen bridges'.

The 3 Billy Goats Gruff (Traditional tale)
A traditional tale which could be used as a stimulus for 'Fallen bridges', where the children could complete the task for the troll or 3 Billy Goats Gruff.

Changes, Changes (Pat Hutchins, 1st Aladdin Books, 1987)
A good book to encourage talk about similarities, differences, shapes, sizes and colours linked to building.

Links to theory

Maria Montessori

Montessori's work was focused on developing main curriculum areas, including language development, number concepts and the exploration of the wider world. She stated that children should be free to choose materials and resources that interest them, within set boundaries. Montessori also recognised the importance of having uninterrupted periods of time to carry out tasks to ensure children had time to explore and complete projects (Pound, 2005). This theory underpins the nature and importance of construction in Early Years settings.

What does this look like in practice?

Practitioners should allow children to plan, negotiate and then carry out small and large constructions without the constraints of time. There should also be opportunities for independent and collaborative work to ensure others have time to join in to develop or improve the structures further and evaluate the work. A variety of resources should also be available on both a large and small scale to encourage a range of building for different contexts.

Making mathematical marks

- Making maps and plans for their constructions
- Writing door numbers on buildings and structures
- Making marks on their constructions
- Simple data handling to show the number of shapes used, etc.
- Making records of their structures and key ideas such as shape, height, length, etc.
- Recording the similarities and differences between structures using marks, sorting or simple tables

5 | Role play

Why role play is important

Role play can be developed inside or outside and on large and small scales. There is a tendency to provide commercial resources for role play such as ready-made costumes and plastic food; however these items tend to have limited uses. This chapter will promote an open-ended and creative approach to role play where 'real' resources are used and where children are involved in equipping and setting up areas. The activities promote the use of cheap or free resources to stimulate children's imaginations and enable play to take off on a whole range of levels. This type of play allows children to immerse themselves in different roles, providing a safe place to take risks, re-enact situations and explore feelings. Effective role play scenarios provide real-life, purposeful contexts for exploring mathematics and making mathematical marks.

Links to other areas of learning

Personal Social and Emotional Development	• Developing social skills as children work together, take turns and share • Encouraging children to express a range of emotions • Helping to develop confidence and self-esteem as children take on roles, face challenges and take risks • Providing children with opportunities to consider and talk about their home lives and communities, and explore those of others • Supporting moral development as children consider what is right or wrong, considering other peoples perspectives

Communication and Language	• Extending vocabulary as children explore language used in different scenarios • Promoting speaking and listening skills
Literacy	• Supporting early reading skills as children access environmental texts • Enabling children to explore writing for an audience and with a purpose • Developing storytelling, exploring plot, sequence of events, setting and characters
Understanding the World	• Exploring concepts relating to time and place, both familiar and unfamiliar, real and fantasy • Providing opportunities for children to learn about the lives and cultures of others • Promoting the relevance of ICT in everyday life
Physical Development	• Developing both large-scale and small-scale movements • Practising dressing and undressing • Exploring the importance of being fit and healthy (e.g. caring for a baby, bedtime routines, going to the doctors, healthy eating)
Expressive Arts and Design	• Developing the imagination, making and designing skills as children develop, plan and organise the area • Communicating and expressing their feelings, ideas and preferences • Developing the imagination as children take on roles, develop storytelling, and imagine how someone else might speak and behave
Mathematics	• Number • Counting • Calculation • Measuring (including time) • Shape and space • Data handling

Key resources

- Cardboard boxes (various shapes and sizes)
- Lengths of different materials
- Hats and bags
- Mark making materials
- Small table and chairs (if required)
- Writing forms relevant to the area
- Clocks (real where possible)
- Posters and signs related to the area
- Real phones (mobiles and land phones)
- Other resources required will be specific to the scenario being explored

Maths web

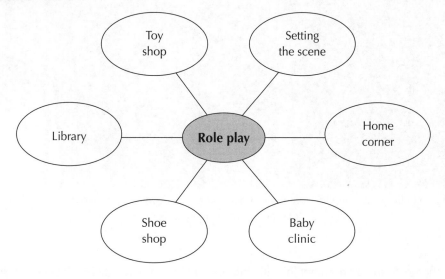

Setting the scene

Before setting up any areas with the children, take time to talk to them about the scenarios. Which type of area would they like to have? Have they been to the place before? What's it like there? Who would they see there and what do they do? What things could they make for the area? Speak to parents/carers and ask for donations of real items to enhance the provision. Where possible organise a group visit to a local example of the scenario, taking photos to help develop the area on your return, and asking for any donations of resources. Involve parents or local members of the community in the development of the area to talk about related occupations or experiences. Practitioners need to take time to model play in the area sensitively, by taking on roles and playing alongside the children.

Home corner

Make-believe play provides numerous opportunities to develop and explore ideas relating to all aspects of mathematical learning.

The 'home' is an environment that all children will be familiar with and have experience of (albeit very different experiences). If space allows, children should ideally always have access to a home corner in addition to a more thematic area. Providing a literacy and numeracy rich environment is crucial. Where possible, real clocks (including alarm clocks), calendars, phones, magazines and timers should be available. The home corner offers an abundance of real-life problem-solving possibilities related to time, daily routine and meal times (including cooking and setting the table for a family meal.) The focus of the play can be enhanced and extended through exploring real-life situations such as planning a surprise birthday party. This could involve planning a party menu for a set number of guests, making birthday banners and cards with ages on, wrapping presents and making invitations. Moving day could provide opportunities to sort objects according to size, type or shape for packing, finding out how many things fit in a box and exploring different sized boxes, as well as physically experiencing 'weight' as boxes are transported. How could the boxes be moved most easily?

Baby clinic

Resource this area with lots of dolls and baby equipment such as high chairs, buggies, toys, baby baths and clothes, as well as real posters and leaflets. Set up a table with a tape measure and scales where babies can be weighed and measured. Provide clipboards where children can record babies' height and weight. A visit from the local health visitor to talk about his or her role would be invaluable. If any parents are happy to bring in young babies, this can be a wonderful learning experience. Photographs displayed of the children as babies and at their current age offer opportunities to discuss similarities, differences and change over time.

Shoe shop

Ask for donations of old shoes and encourage the children to put them in pairs into boxes (include some baby pairs and adult pairs). Allow the children to write their own numerals to indicate sizes and prices. Can they suggest ways of finding out whether a shoe fits? Model how to greet customers, finding out the sort of shoes they are looking for (colour preference and type) and ask children to suggest ways of measuring feet. Talk about organising the shoes. Where would a daddy find shoes or a baby? Ask children about other ways the shoes could be sorted: by gender, colour, material, types of fastening and so on. Pretend lots of customers leave the shoes in a big mess. Can the assistants sort and tidy them?

Library

Set up a library area with the children. Discuss ways of organising the books, such as by size or type. Stick some pieces of blank paper in the front of the books with large grids marked on, provide some date stamps and talk to the children about setting the stamp to date the books. Discuss with the children how many books customers can take out. How are they going to check that people don't take too many? Look at some real library cards and talk about the numbers and barcodes. Challenge children to make their own library cards. Set up a small book sale area where books can be purchased. A visit to a library or from a librarian would enhance this learning further.

Toy shop

Ask children to choose toys from around the room to be in the toy shop. Ask them to think about how they want to organise the shop. Which toys will go together and why? Make some price tags for them to use. Provide catalogues to make posters and signs for the shop showing different types of toys for sale or alternatively provide a range of pictures for children to sort. Take on the role of a customer looking for a gift for a girl/boy, baby/child. Show the children how to use the till and provide a calculator so they can add up prices. Make some pictorial shopping lists for children to use and provide resources for them to make their own lists. Model the use of money in the shop to pay for items and giving change. Set up a sale where all prices are reduced by 1p. How much will things cost now? Can the children alter the price tags?

Main activity 1

Down the market

You will need:

- Table to be the stall
- Boxes or crates for sorting fruit/vegetables
- Mark making resources for making price signs
- Money pouch
- Pennies (real if possible)
- Bags
- Calculator
- Scales
- Some real fruit or vegetables (or alternatively plastic ones or salt dough ones made by the children)

Getting started

Prepare a large box containing the fruit and vegetables. Although impractical to provide solely real fruit and vegetables, some examples would extend play and offer children real sensory experiences of food. Include a letter (from the 'farmer') apologizing that the fruit and vegetables are all mixed up because he only had one box or the tractor journey was very bumpy.

Main activity

Tell the children that they will be setting up a fruit and vegetable stall outside. Tell them that their first delivery of fruit and vegetables will be arriving shortly, delivered by a local farmer. Which fruit and vegetables do they think they might find in the box? Make a list of these and talk about which ones they like and dislike. Read the children the 'farmer's' letter and find out what ideas the children have for sorting the fruit and vegetables. Provide some boxes/crates for the children to sort the produce into. Once the boxes have been sorted, these can be labelled by children. Let the children carry these and ask them which boxes they think will be heavy/light. Arrange the boxes on the stall outside. Talk about prices with the children. How much do they think a banana would cost? What about a potato? Or a bunch of grapes? Provide the resources for children to make their own price signs and posters. Talk to the children about the role of the market stall holder. How can they make sure they get the customers to come over to their stall? Show the children how to call out as a stall holder does. Once the stall is set up spend some time playing with the children taking on the role of the stall holder, calling customers, taking money, adding prices, giving change, weighing and counting produce into bags.

What next?

- Prepare shopping lists featuring numerals next to pictures of produce. Encourage 'customers' to make their own.

- Cut some fruit and vegetables in half and explore which ones make the best prints. Make a drape to go behind or over the stall.

- Explore weighing using the fruit and vegetables. Can the children find any that weigh the same? Which ones are the heaviest and lightest? Extend this by weighing using non-standard units such has cubes, sorting toys or cotton reels. How many does it take to balance a potato? What about a satsuma?

Main activity 2

Up in space

You will need:

- *Ground control*: A table, some chairs, computer keyboards, walkie talkies, mark making resources, note pads, telephones, books about space
- *Space rocket*: A large cardboard box (ideally decorated by the children)
- *Planet*: A large drape on the floor or carpet tiles or paper decorated by the children
- *Astronauts*: Some walkie talkies, cardboard box helmets, space suits, wellies, magnifying glasses

You will also need picture cards showing simple pictures of aliens with varying features: different colours, different-shaped bodies, various numbers of eyes/legs/arms/heads (there should be two identical cards of each alien). Put one set of cards at ground control and a matching set on the planet, face down spread around the planet.

Getting started

Tell the children that they will be having a space adventure today. The astronauts need to get into the spaceship whilst the others go to the ground control area (this should ideally be set up a little way from the rocket and planet.) Ensure that the astronauts and the ground control each have a walkie talkie, and explain that this will be how they will communicate with each other during the trip.

Main activity

Once the astronauts are ready, count down together from 10 to 0, encouraging children to show this on their fingers as they do so. Warn the astronauts that there are reports of aliens on the planet and they need to report back any aliens they find to ground control. Show the astronauts how to moonwalk as they leave their ship and challenge them to take their magnifying glasses and look for aliens on the planet (the cards you have left there earlier). Once they have found an alien encourage them to describe it to ground control using their walkie talkie. Can the children at ground control look at their set of alien cards and work out which ones the children are describing? Once the astronauts have found all the aliens and reported back to ground control, the astronauts may return to their spaceship and count down before returning to Earth.

What next?

- Provide notebooks for ground control to record pictures of the aliens described by the astronauts. The astronauts return with their cards and see if they match the drawings.

- Put numbered pebbles on the planet (these could be moon rocks). Give ground control a set of matching number cards and choose numbers at random for the astronauts to collect in a bucket and return to Earth with. Match numbers and pebbles on their return. Extend this by asking astronauts to find 'one more than...' or 'one less than...'

- Use chalk to draw some numbered planets outside. Ground control rolls a dice and tells the astronauts which planets to visit. Journeys could be recorded by drawing lines and linking planets. After a few goes the astronauts and ground control swap over. Mark the journey in a different colour. Did the second group take the same route? Did they visit any of the same planets? Were there any planets both or neither groups visited?

Look, listen and note

- How do children count out objects from a larger group?
- How are children beginning to represent numbers?
- Are they able to talk about how they sort and arrange items?
- Can they identify simple problems in role play contexts and talk about how they might solve them?
- How do children use mathematical tools to help them solve problems?

❓ Key questions

- How are we going to solve this problem?
- What shall we try first/next?
- What would happen if . . .?
- What could we use to help us?
- Can we think of a different/better/easier way?

Key vocabulary

Counting: Number, zero, one, two, three up to ten, how many, count

Calculating: Add, more, altogether, one more, two more, take away, one less, two less

Solving problems: Sort, group, set, match, same, different, find, choose

Using money: Money, coin, penny, pence, pound, price, cost, buy, sell, spend, pay, change, expensive, cheap, total

Time: Days of the week, morning, afternoon, evening, night, bedtime, dinnertime, hour, o'clock

Health and safety

- Remind the children to keep the area tidy as items on the floor can present trip hazards.
- Children need to be reminded not to put small objects such as coins into their mouths.
- Batteries in equipment should be regularly changed and checked for leakage.

Useful stories and rhymes

The Baby's Catalogue (Allan & Janet Ahlberg, Puffin, 1984)

Miss Polly had a dolly (Traditional rhyme)
Links to the baby clinic and is a good starting point for talking about keeping healthy and babies.

Whatever Next? (Jill Murphy, Macmillan Children's Books, 2007)
Links well to the space theme, constructing rockets and making astronaut outfits.

Aliens Love Underpants (Claire Freeman & Ben Cort, Simon & Schuster Children's Books, 2007)
Links to space and aliens, offering opportunities to explore shape, colour and pattern.

Biggest Bed in the World (Lindsay Camp and Jonathan Langley, HarperCollins Children's Books, 2000)

Ten in the bed (traditional counting rhyme)
Link well to homes and families. How many people can fit into a bed before they either fall out or the bed becomes too full/heavy?

This is Our House (Michael Rosen and Bob Graham, Walker Books, 2007)
Links to sorting and counting.

Just Like Jasper (Mick Inkpen and Nick Butterworth, Hodder Children's Books, 1990)
Links to the toy shop, spending money, counting, sorting and position.

Links to theory

Tina Bruce

Tina Bruce is a contemporary theorist who advocates a free-flow, child-led approach to play. Drawing on the work of key theorists, a range of evidence and her own research she identified '12 features of free flow play' (Bruce 2004). She identified the power of role play as a vehicle for children to imagine other places, times and people. Bruce expressed the belief that when 7 or more of these 12 key features were evident within children's play, there was an increased likelihood of valuable learning taking place. The majority of the features revolve around the importance of child-initiated play, relationships and interactions, all crucial elements of any effective role play provision.

What does this look like in practice?

The most effective role play scenarios are developed around children's interests and experiences. Children should be involved in the planning and resourcing of areas, promoting a sense of involvement and engagement. Role play should provide opportunities to re-enact and rehearse real-life experiences as well as opportunities to imagine and explore fantasy worlds. Effective practitioners follow the children's lead during role play, engaging and becoming a part of the play when welcomed, without dominating play. They are tuned into the children enough to recognise when adult-free play is needed.

Making mathematical marks

- Involve children in making signs and resources such as posters, opening and closing time lists and price tags.

- Provide real diaries, appointment books, telephone directories, timetables, menus, and model how to use these.

- Provide clipboards and pencils for children to work out totals when selling items in the shop or on the stall and model simple ways of working out totals using pictures and tallies.

- Talk about 'stock taking' and provide forms with pictures of items down one side (for example, apple, banana and potato for the market stall). Ask children to record how many of each they have in stock. What do they need to get more of?

6 Creative workshop

Why the creative workshop is important

This area encompasses a whole range of media and materials for children to explore and be creative with, such as paint, messy play, cutting, sticking, drawing, textiles, sculpture, mosaic, junk modelling and printing. When children work in this area they naturally explore shape and space in both 2 and 3 dimensions on large and small scales. It is important the creative workshop is an area full of interesting resources for children to choose freely from, such as fabric, boxes, recycled materials, sequins, glitter and a range of mark making materials, tools and equipment.

Links to other areas of learning

Personal Social and Emotional Development	• Developing independence as children select tools and resources • Promoting high levels of involvement, engagement and perseverance • Encouraging children to work together, share and take turns • Developing children's confidence and self-esteem • Offering opportunities to learn about rules, boundaries and personal safety
Communication and Language	• Encouraging children to talk about their ideas, decisions and methods • Extending vocabulary as children name and describe the resources on offer and use language associated with them • Encouraging children to talk through their learning, negotiating and interacting with others as they work

Literacy	• Developing essential pre writing skills as children use a range of large and small tools and equipment • Encouraging children to make marks and give meanings to them • Opportunities to develop reading by providing simple labels including pictures and text to support children as they access and return resources
Understanding the World	• Investigating materials and comparing their properties, similarities and differences • Using resources to represent the local environment through junk modelling and simple map making
Physical Development	• Promoting the development of fine and gross motor skills as children work on small and large scales • Helping children learn to use tools safely and correctly • Developing hand–eye coordination
Expressive Arts and Design	• Providing opportunities to explore how tools work such as a stapler, a hole punch and scissors • Developing designing and making skills; joining together, constructing, adapting, building, evaluating • Providing opportunities to consider the use of tools for a purpose • Allowing children to express and communicate their ideas, feelings and thoughts • Offering opportunities for children to explore new media and materials • Encouraging children to explore colour, shape, space and form to create on both large and small scales • Stimulating the imagination, and encouraging children to represent ideas, thoughts and feelings using a range of resources and equipment
Mathematics	• Measuring • Number • Size • Counting • Calculating • Matching and sorting • Shape • Pattern • Position and direction

Key resources

- Pencils, pens, crayons, pastels, paints, chalks, etc.
- Paintbrushes, sponges and rollers
- Different sizes and types of paper
- Glue sticks and PVA glue
- Fabric of different types and in varying sizes, including large pieces for dressing up and tent making
- Wrapping paper and recycled greeting cards
- Sticky tape, masking tape
- Hole punch, stapler, scissors
- Glitter, sequins, buttons, cotton reels, corks and collections of other items

Maths web

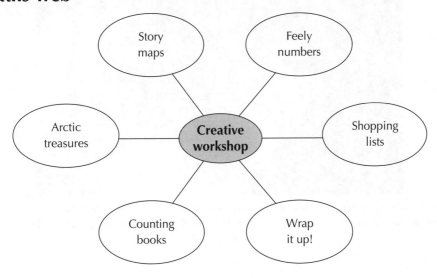

Feely numbers

Prepare some number outlines on coloured card, preferably A4 sized, or provide some large templates for children to draw around to make their own numbers. Explain that they will be making some feely numbers for a game and ask them to choose what they would like to fill their number with from the resources on offer (these need to be tactile objects such as buttons, shells, sequins, pieces of furry or rough material, sandpaper, dried pasta, rice, split peas, lentils or beans). Do they think that they will need a lot or

Providing a range of mark making materials encourages children to make their own mathematical marks; the addition of number templates provides images of numbers for children to explore.

a little to fill their number? This could lead to discussions around how fewer larger pieces would be needed (for example pasta tubes) whereas lots of smaller pieces (such as grains of rice or lentils) would be needed. Encourage the children to fill their numbers completely whilst modelling everyday language to reinforce correct formation of the number, for example: round, down, back, across, up, around and straight. Once the numbers are finished and dried, challenge children to close their eyes and work out which number they can feel. These feely numerals are also great for displays and hiding around the setting for number hunts.

Shopping lists

Provide some catalogues for the children to cut pictures from to make their own shopping lists. Encourage children to cut out items and stick them onto paper. They could then decide how much each item costs and make their own mathematical marks to indicate cost. Talk to the children about the most expensive and cheapest items on their list. Added to the role play area, these lists would help show the importance of money in real-life situations whilst giving the children a sense of ownership and pride as their resources become a valuable part of play. In a world where children often see cards being used to pay for items, where shopping is often done virtually, and during these times of global financial difficulty, the handling of coins (real where possible) to explore the concepts of buying and selling has never been more important!

Wrap it up!

Tell the children that they are going to be giving presents to each other. Children can choose toys from around the classroom. (Remind them that these will be returned afterwards!) Can the children find boxes that will hold their presents? Encourage them to look at the boxes on offer and talk about their shape and size and allow them time to explore the different-sized ones. Which box is the biggest? Smallest? Are any the same shape and size? Once they have found the correct-sized box, challenge them to find a piece of paper to wrap it in. Make sure you have a variety of paper available, including some that would clearly be far too small or too big. Encourage the children to try out different sized paper until they find the right piece. Children could also look at some wrapping paper and talk about the patterns then try to make their own by printing with everyday objects.

Counting books

Prepare some simple booklets by folding some A4 paper and stapling it (older children could do this themselves, choosing how many pages they will need, folding the paper lengthways or widthways and choosing the best tool to secure it with). Ask the children to decide which numbers they would like in their books; you could either write these for them, provide templates to draw around, or simply encourage the children to have a go at writing their own numbers. Ask them to choose from the resources on the table (buttons, pasta, sequins, beans, peas) and stick the correct number of items on to each page. Once the books are made, share these together and use them to help children practise counting.

Arctic treasure

Prepare a large tray of shaving foam or shredded paper and hide varying numbers of objects within it. Small items such as glass pebbles, buttons, conkers, shells, plastic cubes and pegs are ideal for this; however, ideally try to hide only 4 or 5 different types of item. Provide whiteboards for the explorers to record their treasure on. Explain to the children that you have just heard on the news that there is some treasure hidden in the Arctic. Ask them how they could keep track of what they find. How will they remember? Encourage the children to explore the shaving foam/shredded paper and record a mark next on their board each time they find something. After 5 minutes look at everyone's lists. What did they find the most/fewest of? To develop this activity children could hide a piece of treasure and guide a friend to it using 'hotter' and 'colder' as they approach or move away from it.

Story maps

This activity works well when linked with stories based around a journey such as *Rosie's Walk* by Pat Hutchins or *We're Going on a Bear Hunt* by Michael Rosen. Roll out some wallpaper and attach this to a table or hard floor area with masking tape. Explain to the children that they will be working together to make a special map. Look at the story together and talk about the different places in the story. Where does the story start and finish? Encourage the children to make a map relating to the chosen story, using the boxes, containers and other recycled materials as landmarks within the story and drawing paths and other features on the map. Once the map is completed use some small world figures to re-enact the story, encouraging children to move the characters along the map from the beginning of the story to the end, talking about where they go first, next, after, before as well as what they go past, over, under, through, above and so on. These maps can also be used for child-initiated small world play and can also be linked to the local environment, providing opportunities for children to talk about their own journeys.

Main activity 1

Patchwork blankets
You will need:

- Various-sized soft toys
- Roll of wallpaper or large pieces of paper
- Shapes cut out of fabrics or pieces of fabric

- Shape templates
- Scissors
- Markers
- Glue and sticky tape

Getting started

Talk to the children about patchwork blankets. Have they seen any before? What did they look like? Find some pictures of patchwork blankets (or even better some actual blankets) to show the children. Explain to the children that the soft toys (try to provide various-sized toys) in the setting have been feeling quite cold at night and need some blankets to keep them warm.

Main activity

Provide a roll of wallpaper and ask each child to cut a piece long enough to cover the toy. This will be the base for the blanket. Ask the children how they can find out how big the blankets need to be and model measuring them directly on the toys if necessary, talking about whether they are too big, too small or just right! Challenge them to design their own blankets. Either provide a range of patches cut from different materials (in various shapes such as a circle, square, rectangle and triangle) or provide cardboard templates for the children to draw round to make their own fabric patches. The type of art paper that has white paper on one side and a fabric-type material on the other is ideal for this, as children can easily draw around their template on the paper side before cutting it out. Before children glue their patches on, allow them time to explore the shapes and find the best way of covering their blankets. Do any of them organise their shapes by fitting them together systematically or do they randomly place them all over the paper? Once they are happy that their blankets are ready they can glue the patches on. How many patches have they used so far? How many more do they think they will need? Which shapes do they want to use? Do they choose all of one shape (e.g. squares) or do they use a variety of shapes? Which ones fit together well? Which ones leave gaps between them letting a draft through to the poor chilly toys? Once the children have made blankets these can be looked at and compared. What is the same and different about them? Which one is biggest/smallest? Which one has the most/fewest patches on it? Which toy do they think would need the biggest/smallest blanket and why?

What next?

- The blankets could form the basis for a simple data handling activity where the number of shapes used could be recorded by tally marks and compared. If children have used a range of shapes they could investigate which shape they used most/least.

- Provide the children with some shape dice featuring triangle, square, rectangle, circle, hexagon and '?' for 'you choose'. Children take it in turns to roll the dice and collect the correct shape to put onto their blanket. This could be done on a large or small scale using prepared fabric shapes, shape stampers or shape sponges. Small mosaic pattern blocks would also work well.

Main activity 2

If the hat fits . . .
You will need:

- Various length strips of paper
- Staplers, glue, sticky tape, rulers, crayons, pens, collage materials

Getting started

Explain to the children that they will be making hats for each other. Provide the children with a range of paper strips of varying lengths (including some that would be too short or far too long for a hat) and thicknesses.

Main activity

Speak to the children and find out what ideas they have for making their hats. How do they think they could make the strips into hats? How are they going to make sure that the hats will fit? Allow the children some time to try out their own ideas for measuring strips and if necessary model how to measure a child's head using some of the strips of paper to wrap round into a crown. Choose some strips that are obviously far too short and ask the children which ones they think will be long enough. Once the children have chosen the correct length of paper, they could explore measuring by finding out how many pencils, cubes or sorting objects fit along it. Who has the longest length of paper? For younger children the strips could be measured by direct comparison; which one is longest or shortest? Children can decorate their hats by drawing, colouring or painting. Alternatively children could roll a numbered dice (either 1–3 or 1–6) and stick or print the correct number of items onto it. Once the children have decorated their strips, provide sticky tape, glue sticks, PVA glue with spreaders and a stapler. Which one will they choose to secure their hat with and why? If using tape, can they cut/tear the correct length?

What next?

- Children could make hats for some soft toys, predicting which one will need the longest or shortest strip for a hat. Once a few hats have been made, these could be muddled up and children could be challenged to match a hat to each toy before a timer runs out.

- Children could choose number cards and stick the correct number of objects onto their hats. They could then record the correct numerals on the hats by using a template or recording their own numerals. These could then be used to support counting, ordering and number rhyme activities.

- Provide a coloured dice or spinner. Children could roll the dice or spin the spinner and stick something of the same colour onto their hats. This could be made more challenging by providing a range of coloured sticky shapes and 2 dice: one with the correlating shapes, one with the correlating colours. Children have to roll both dice and find the correct shape to stick on, for example a red triangle, blue square and so on.

Look, listen and note

- How are children beginning to represent numbers?
- Are they using their developing ideas to solve problems in practical contexts?
- How do they count out objects from a bigger group of objects?
- What ideas do they have about why something is the correct size? How do they try to find this out?
- Do they use mathematical language to describe shapes and name them?
- Do they use positional and directional language?

? Key questions

- What's the same/different about those buttons/pieces of material/shapes/boxes?
- How many or how much do you think you will need to use?
- How could we record what you have done so we don't forget?
- Can you tell you friend about what you have made?
- What could you try next?

Key vocabulary

Counting: Count, 1, 2, 3 up to 10 and beyond, more, less, same, different

Measures: Measure, length, width, height, long, short, tall, thick, thin

Shape: (3D) cube, pyramid, sphere, cone; (2D) circle, triangle, square, rectangle, star, oval

Pattern: Pattern, repeating pattern, match, same

Position: Over, under, above, below, top, bottom, side, on, in, around, in front, behind, front, back

Health and safety

- The creative workshop is a treasure trove of small interesting objects. Adults need to remind children not to put objects into their mouths, up nostrils or into ears and ensure adequate supervision.
- Children should be encouraged to use tools and equipment independently, but adults need to ensure children are taught these skills safely and correctly, especially in relation to scissors and other cutting tools, staplers, hole punches and other everyday tools. Adults should remind children about the safe use and handling of these tools.
- The creative workshop can easily become messy and items on the floor present a trip hazard. Children need to be taught to tidy their work space, ensuring any waste is disposed of and any items on the floor are picked up.

📖 Useful stories and rhymes

Baa baa black sheep (Traditional rhyme)
Could be developed to incorporate other colours and materials e.g. blue cotton, red silk and so on.

I can sing a rainbow
Links to colours and could be used to support activities based around sequencing and patterns.

Rosie's Walk (Pat Hutchins, Random Century, 1968)

We're Going on a Bear Hunt (Michael Rosen and Helen Oxenbury, Walker Books, 1989)

The Shopping Basket (John Burningham, Red Fox, 1992)
These stories provide opportunities to talk about journeys (including directional and positional language and environmental features) and would support simple map making activities.

Elmer the Elephant (David McKee, Anderson Press, 1989)
Links to activities around colour, pattern, shapes and patchwork.

Links to theory

Guy Claxton

Claxton is a contemporary theorist who believes that there is too much focus on the traditional Rs relating to literacy and numeracy and not enough focus on the 4 Rs that he believes are important for stimulating the brain: Resilience, Reflection, Reciprocity and Resourcefulness. Claxton has also written at length about creativity and its diverse and individual nature and how practitioners can support this area. He has suggested eight Is linked to creativity: Immersion, Inquisitiveness, Investigation, Interaction, Imagination, Intuition, Intellect and Imitation (Pound 2009).

What does this look like in practice?

The eight Is listed above seem to sum up all that the creative workshop area should stimulate and promote in any good Early Years setting. Claxton's ideas about stimulating children's imagination, curiosity and opportunities to explore and investigate are all offered in abundance in a well-stocked and rich workshop area. Practitioners should operate as role models in the workshop area as identified in one of Claxton's Is: Imitation. By making time to play and learn alongside children, modelling the safe and correct use of tools and equipment and even allowing children to see how their own creative ideas develop, practitioners can play a vital role in supporting young children's creativity.

Making mathematical marks

- Provide a wide range of mark making tools and equipment for children to use to make their own marks for the activities outlined above and their own self-initiated activities.

- Provide number shapes and templates for children to choose from.

- Provide a range of small objects for children to print with such as buttons, corks, blocks and so on.

- Powder paint is a great resource as children are able to measure their own powder and water, make choices about colours and develop pre-writing skills as they mix and explore their paints.

7 Small world

Why small world play is important

This type of play is a favourite with children as they have opportunities to explore different and imaginative worlds and characters. Resources such as the train set, cars and garage, animals, doll's house and toy castle offer a wealth of mathematical concepts such as counting, sorting, adding and subtracting, matching, measuring and problem solving. This type of play along with construction is often a favourite with boys and the perfect way in to support, assess and extend their learning in real contexts. Children feel confident when working in an imaginative world and will therefore work with greater confidence when using and applying mathematics in this area of provision.

Links to other areas of learning

Personal Social and Emotional Development	• Providing opportunities to work together and share resources • Solving problems and undertaking self-chosen challenges to create their own small world play environments • Making links between different parts of their life and experiences, for example using a hospital to talk about their own visit to see a doctor
Communication and Language	• Communicating with others to negotiate plans or share ideas • Imaginative play using a range of resources provided by adults and made by children themselves • Developing a wealth of vocabulary to talk about their own experiences linked to small world play

Literacy	• Orally telling stories or retelling familiar events
	• Stories and rhymes linked to small world play settings, for example the farm and the hospital
	• Giving meaning to marks or writing for a purpose, for example making road signs for the car roadway or train station
	• Writing imaginative stories linked to small world play such as castles, space stations, train journeys or under the water
Understanding the World	• Talking about features of objects, for example trains, cars or farm machinery
	• Talking about and remembering past experiences from their lives and their feelings linked to these experiences
	• Making maps of small world scenarios including those they have first hand experience of and also those they do not. These can be used for play mats.
Physical Development	• Cutting skills to make resources for the small world environment
	• Using paintbrushes, pencils or crayons to create scenery for the small world environments
	• Using a range of tools to make changes to materials to create effects for small world play scenery or resources
Expressive Arts and Design	• Planning a small world environment for animals, people or buildings, thinking about what they will need and how they will make it
	• Linking experiences to designing and making objects for small world play and joining materials using simple techniques
	• Songs linked to small world play settings, for example 'Old Macdonald' and 'Miss Polly had a dolly'
	• Painting scenery for the small world play equipment to put in a tray or on a table
	• Using junk modelling resources to create a small world play environment such as playground equipment for a park
	• Using instruments for sounds linked to the small world play, for example for the weather or animal sounds
	• Expressing and communicating their ideas, thoughts and feelings through imaginative play
	• Playing alongside other children engaged in the same small world theme, using their imagination
	• Beginning to introduce a story or narrative to their imaginative play

Mathematics	• Numbers
	• Counting
	• Calculating
	• Shape
	• Measures – height
	• Direction/position
	• Sorting and matching

Key resources

- Large paper such as rolls of wallpaper
- Cars, garage, car mats/tracks
- Train sets (wooden and plastic) with a range of track pieces (straight and curved) and different-sized trains
- Doll's house with furniture and dolls
- Farm with a range of farm animals, tractors, farm objects such as hay bales, sty, coop, scarecrow
- Castle with knights, shields, drawbridge, horses, flags, king and queen characters
- Dinosaurs

Maths web

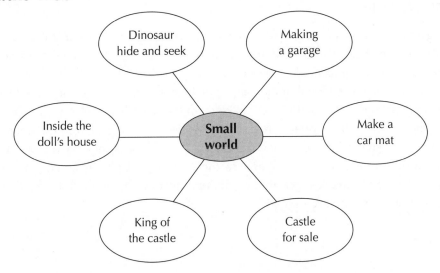

Making a garage

Use masking tape to make a garage for cars by marking out different-shaped spaces (children could help to plan this and tear the tape to create the correct-shaped spaces). Provide sticky labels/number cards for children to number the cars and garage spaces using mathematical marks or number labels. Can the children match the correct cars to the spaces? How many cars are there in the garage today? What if two of the cars are taken for repairs, how many will be left? Discuss the repairs that take place in the garage and the equipment used, for example the lifting platform; can the children describe the direction it moves in and what happens to the car on the platform? Provide simple writing frames for garage work, for example recording the number of cars they are working on and the registration plates of these cars.

Make a car mat

Give the children a selection of different-sized and coloured cars. Explain that they have the cars but the car mat has gone missing. Can they make their own? Encourage children to use marks, including straight and curved lines to create a map of a town or city for the cars to travel around. What shapes will they use for buildings? Bridges? Ponds? Provide a range of flat shapes for children to use as templates and talk about what they could use for each part of the map. Allow plenty of time for children to use their cars on the map. Listen to and encourage talk about the position of their cars on the map and directions to go to buildings or areas on the map. How could they record the directions or the route their cars are taking?

Castle for sale

A king and a princess are looking for a new castle to move into. There are none for sale, can the children help? What could they use to build a castle? Talk about the position of the bricks, blocks or junk modelling resources they are using. Discuss what will happen if they build one turret too tall if they are using blocks. Are the walls the same height? How do they know? How could they make them the same height? How many people are going to live in the castle? Where will they sleep? How many rooms should the castle have? What shapes can they see on the bricks/blocks they have used? What shape are the rooms in their castle? Use the small world play characters to allow imaginative play in the castle. Can the children think of any more problems that the king or princess might have to solve?

The king of the castle

Use the castles that children have built for the 'Castle for sale' activity. Explain that the king and the princess are pleased with their castle but now want to decorate it to make it look like their home. What would a castle need? Explore making flags; how can they make sure that each side of the flag looks the same? Use printing for repeating patterns, shapes and colours on the flags. Talk about how many flags would be needed; can the children organise the correct number to be made and choose the correct number of resources, such as straws, paper? Talk about the furniture that would be needed for the castle such as thrones, beds and chairs. Can the children use small 3D shapes to make the furniture for the castle? What shapes have they used? Can they record how many shapes they have used by using numerals or marks next to pictures of the 3D shapes?

Inside the doll's house

Provide children with an empty doll's house and a box of doll's house furniture. Explain that it is their job to set up the doll's house, but before the furniture is put into the house it needs to be sorted out so that each item is put into the correct room. Give children simple pictures of a bedroom, a kitchen, a bathroom and a lounge in sorting circles. Can the children sort the furniture into the correct sorting ring? Talk about which room has the most/fewest pieces of furniture. Ask them to label the sorting circles with marks, numerals or number cards to show how many pieces of furniture there are for each room. Ask them then to put the furniture in each room of the house and ask questions about what they are doing such as 'How many beds are there?' and 'How many people could sleep in the house?' Ask the children to put the pictures used for sorting into 4 boxes and sort the furniture into these boxes when the doll's house is tidied away to make sure it doesn't get mixed up again.

Dinosaur hide and seek

Use a large tray with green and brown fabric or paper in the bottom of it. Leave a set of plastic dinosaurs in the tray. Explain to the children that the dinosaurs are playing hide and seek; the tall dinosaurs like to hide in the trees (green) and the short dinosaurs always hide in the swamp (brown). Can the children hide the dinosaurs in the right place? Look at how they sort the dinosaurs; do they compare the dinosaurs by holding them side by side? Provide children with some interlocking cubes and ask them to make some more dinosaurs for the game of hide and seek. Can they make tall dinosaurs to hide in the trees and shorter ones for the swamp? Talk about their choices and which dinosaur is the tallest/shortest in the tray. How will they know?

New dimensions can be added to small world play through the introduction of interesting natural objects and resources that support children to explore 3D shape and space.

 ## Main activity 2

The train ride

You will need:

- Plastic/wooden train track pieces (straight and curved)
- Trains with carriages that can be filled with characters
- Tunnels
- Small world people or animals
- Paper/card

Getting started

Sing a song or read a story about trains. Have the children ever gone on a train journey? Act out a train ride using actions and sounds. Show children the small world people/animals in train carriages (from a train track set). Explain that people/animals have gone on a train journey but during their journey they have run out of track. What can the children do to help?

Main activity

Allow children to use real pieces of track or make their own pieces of track to solve the problem. If they make their own pieces, talk about the shape and size of the pieces that they will need. Talk about the similarities and differences between train track pieces, highlighting the language 'straight' and 'curved'. Once the children have selected their pieces allow them to continue the track. Pose questions such as 'What if they get to a river/pond?', 'What if there's a tunnel in their way?', 'How many pieces might they need to reach . . .?', 'What type of pieces might they need?', 'How could we build a square train track?', 'Can we make a circular one?', 'Which pieces would we need?' to extend their thinking. Observe how they solve the problems and ask them to talk about their choices and explain their thinking. Once the track has been built, allow children to use it with the carriages for small world play. Discuss how many animals/people they will have going on their journey and how many they will put into each train carriage. Will all the carriages have the same number of characters in them? Encourage the children to talk through their journey such as 'the train is inside the tunnel', 'the train is beside the pond' and 'it is going in a straight line'.

What next?

- Provide a greater number of empty carriages for the train journey and pose questions such as 'If every carriage has two people in, how many people will be going on the journey?' or 'If you have got ten people, how many could be in each carriage?'

- Give children pictures of different-shaped train tracks such as square, rectangular or circular. Can the children choose the correct pieces to enable them to make a track that is the same shape as the picture? Can they describe the pieces they have chosen?

- Give the children a set number of pieces such as 10 or 20 and explain that these are the only pieces they have. What track can they make? Is it the same as or different from someone else's that has the same number of pieces?

Main activity 2

On the farm

You will need:

- A range of farm animals including parents and their young
- A farm
- Paper and clipboards
- Mark making resources

Getting started

Sing a song or counting rhyme that is based around farm animals. Explain to the children that the farmer is having trouble at the farm. He is not very good at counting and he doesn't know if he has all the animals in the right places. Can they help him? Talk about the strategies children could use to help the farmer.

Main activity

Let the children have time using the farm animals and farm to solve the farmer's problem. Talk to them about their choices and the methods they are using. Look to see if children are sorting the animals by type, animal families or where they would be found on the farm. Suggest ideas linked to sorting the animals by type and putting them onto the farm where they would live. As the children are doing this, encourage them to count how many of each type there are on the farm. Once the children have sorted all the animals, ask them how they will let the farmer know how many of each animal there are to help him with his counting. Allow the children to try out their ideas and note how they choose to represent their findings; do they use numerals, marks or drawings? Help children to create a simple table to present their findings with pictures of animals in one column and room for children to record the number of each type in the other column. Ask questions such as 'How many horses are there?', 'Are there more pigs or cows on the farm?'

What next?

- Prompt simple calculations using the farm animals such as asking children how they would work out how many cows and horses are in the field altogether. Support the combining of groups and modelling simple number sentences (as appropriate).

- Challenge children to find the correct number of animals to make a total, using problems such as 'The farmer has 10 animals on the farm. What animals could he have?'
- Encourage children to record their sorting of animals on the farm. How could they present this? Through drawings? Recording using numerals/marks?

Look, listen and note

- What language are they using as they explore counting and calculating?
- Are they able to find the correct number of objects to make a given total?
- Can they add two sets by combining them?
- Can they talk about their ideas when they are solving problems?
- Do they use correct mathematical language when describing shapes or the position of objects?

? Key questions

- How many are there altogether?
- What shapes can you see?
- Can you explain how you solved the problem?
- What could you try next?
- How could you count these objects to check how many there are?
- What will you choose? Why?

Key vocabulary

Counting: Number, zero, one, two, three up to ten, how many, count, more, less, many, few, guess how many, estimate, many, few

Calculating: Add, more, and, make, total, altogether, take (away), is the same as, take (away), leave, how many more to make . . .? How many more is . . . than . . .? How many are left/left over?

Solving problems: Sort, order, same, different, find, choose, collect, use, make, tell me, describe, talk about, explain, draw, record, same, different

Measures: Measure, size, compare, enough, not enough, too much, too little, too many, too few, nearly, height, short, tall, shorter, taller, shortest, tallest

Patterns: Symmetrical, pattern, repeating pattern, match

Shape: Face, side, edge, end, flat, curved, straight, round, hollow, solid, corner; (3D) cube, pyramid, sphere, cone; (2D) circle, triangle, square, rectangle, star, oval

Position: Over, under, above, below, top, bottom, side, on, in, in front, behind

⊞ Health and safety

- Ensure children are supervised when cutting to make resources for small world environments.
- Ensure there are no small removable pieces that children could put into their mouths.

📖 Useful stories and rhymes

Old King Cole (Traditional rhyme)

Sing a song of sixpence (Traditional rhyme)
Rhymes to introduce small world play using castles.

Old Macdonald (Traditional song)

Rosie's Walk (Pat Hutchins, Red Fox, 2009)
A favourite song and a picture book to use as a starting point for small world play on the farm.

Oi! Get off Our Train (John Burningham, Red Fox, 1991)

The Train Ride (June Crebbin, Walker Books, 1996)
Two popular picture books to inspire small world play using the train track.

Links to theory

Lev Vygotsky

During small world play activities, children can often exhibit the confidence and enthusiasm that they do not show in other areas of provision in the setting. Vygotsky's work acknowledges the importance of imaginative play as a key to social interaction and child development. It is through play that children can, Vygotsky believes, work beyond their current ability and develop language (Bruce 2004).

It is therefore essential that all children have opportunities to participate in and develop through imaginative play in Early Years settings.

What does this look like in practice?

Practitioners should provide a range of small world play, linked to both familiar and new experiences for children. Familiar experiences such as hospitals, airports, schools, train tracks and doll's houses give children the opportunity to re-enact situations they have experienced themselves or talked about with their families. These can therefore give children the confidence to play and develop language with their peers as they are comfortable with the themes of the small world environment. However, it is also vital to allow children to explore the realms of their imagination through small world play activities based outside of their experiences, such as space stations, underwater, dinosaurs or castles, as they then have the freedom to explore play where any idea can be accepted and explored. Alongside role play this is a key area of provision for young children to share and develop their own ideas and imaginative thinking within settings and these will be areas that children will return to over and over again.

Making mathematical marks

- Making numbers and signs to accompany small world play, for example for the garage, car mats and the farm
- Recording sorting or counting using numerals or marks
- Beginning to write simple number sentences
- Making marks to represent the shapes or direction for car or train journeys

8 | Food and cookery

Why food and cookery are important

This chapter will focus on the use of food and cookery to develop children's early mathematical ideas in a range of exciting ways. Children are fascinated with cooking and especially enjoy eating their wares! The process of cooking, especially when following a recipe, is full of mathematical learning: weighing, timing, capacity and the language of time. Even when the food is made, the learning goes on as children explore sharing, cutting in half, and problem solving. Is there enough for everyone or do we need to make more? This is a key stimulus in Early Years settings as it demonstrates to the children how learning is linked together and the real-life application of their learnt skills.

Links to other areas of learning

Personal Social and Emotional Development	• Sharing time with family and friends during meals to talk about interests, home and their community • Developing table manners when eating at home or in other settings • Opportunities to select and use appropriate resources • Taking turns, sharing and considering needs of others • Developing confidence when trying new foods and expressing their feelings about it
Communication and Language	• Questioning what happens to ingredients when they are cooked or cooled • Talking about their ideas during cooking, for example choices of ingredients, decorating food and choice of implements • Negotiating plans with others when cooking, such as who will mix or who will add ingredients

Literacy	• Reading, listening to and writing simple recipes
	• Stories and rhymes about food and cooking
	• Looking at recipe books and non fiction books to find out more about food
	• Making collages of letters using food such as pasta, beans and lentils to reinforce correct letter formation

Understanding the World	• Identifying similarities and differences between ingredients, foods or shops
	• Talking about the changes that happen during cooking, for example what happens to ingredients when they are mixed, how raw ingredients change when they are cooked or cooled
	• Investigating foods using their senses of touch, taste, smell and sight
	• Finding out about foods from around the world, where food comes from and how the food is eaten
	• Learning about special foods for different religions for celebrations such as Christmas, Easter, Passover, Diwali, birthdays and weddings

Physical Development	• Considering healthy food and lifestyles
	• Using a range of cooking implements safely such as blunt knives, forks, peelers, mashers and graters
	• Working hygienically by washing hands and implements thoroughly before and after cooking and washing fresh foods before eating
	• Exploring a range of movements safely involved in cooking, such as squashing, mashing, cutting, stirring, rolling, patting and kneading
	• Assessing risks before cooking by making rules, such as only adults use the oven, knives to be handled safely, water to be warm not boiling hot for washing up

Expressive Arts and Design	• Singing songs about food and cooking and creating movements linked to food such as long runner beans or small round peas
	• Looking at patterns and colour in a range of food
	• Using a range of media to complete representations of food such as paint, pastels, charcoal, collage resources and crayons
	• Talking about art made using food to create images

Mathematics	
	• Capacity
	• Weight
	• Time
	• Shape
	• Number
	• Calculating

Key resources

- A range of cooking implements – spoons, forks, blunt knives, chopping boards, grater, peeler, cutters, rolling pins
- A range of different-sized bowls and containers
- A variety of food and ingredients
- Shopping bags
- Timers and clocks
- Measuring equipment – cups, measuring spoons, jugs, scales, balances

Maths web

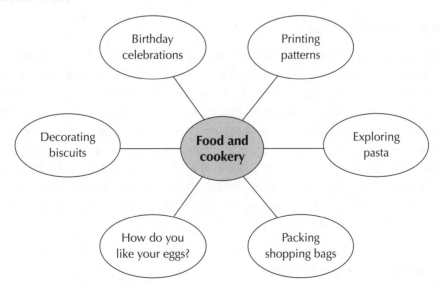

Printing patterns

Provide children with a range of fruit and vegetables. Cut the fruit into halves. Talk about the shapes they can see and the size of each fruit and vegetable. Allow the children to use the fruit and vegetables to make patterns by printing. Give time to make pictures and patterns to explore the marks that are made by each fruit or vegetable. Provide a range of repeating colour or food patterns for children to continue or copy. Talk about what they notice about the patterns, can they talk about the colours or the order of the food? Model ordinal language and the language of comparison such as 'the same as' and 'different from'.

Exploring pasta

Show the children a range of different-shaped and sized dried pasta. Tip this into a large tray and allow children time to explore the shapes, encouraging them to sort them into bowls for dinner. Look at how they choose to sort the pasta and prompt them to count the number of pieces they have in each bowl. If a range of different-sized bowls are put into the tray children can then explore which bowl will hold the most pasta. Talk to the children as they play, posing questions such as 'Which one do you think will hold the most/least?', 'How many pieces of pasta will it hold?', 'How full is your container?', 'How many pieces of pasta will these two containers hold altogether?', 'What shapes can you see?', 'Which is the smallest/biggest?'

Packing shopping bags

Provide children with a range of boxes, tins and containers of food from the supermarket. Explain that you have been shopping and have bought this food but are unsure about how to pack the shopping bags as you're worried that the lighter items will get squashed. Provide them with a range of balances and scales. Let them explore the items to pack and watch how they undertake the problem. Leave some clipboards with paper or pictures of shopping bags to allow them to record what they have done using pictures or mathematical marks. Talk to them about the objects to find out how they know which is heavier or lighter and how they will pack the bag. Ask questions such as 'Is the biggest object the heaviest?', 'How many objects are they putting in each bag?', 'Which bag has more/less?', 'Which bag is the heaviest/lightest?'

How do you like your eggs?

Ask children if they have eaten eggs at home. Talk about how eggs can be cooked in different ways. Cook the eggs by poaching, boiling and scrambling. The children are to measure an amount of scrambled egg to eat each, for example 4 teaspoons, and to have a boiled and poached egg to try. Discuss how to find out who does and doesn't like each type of egg and which type is the children's favourite. Use picture cards or children's photos to make sorting diagrams for the children to show if they like the eggs or not using smiley and sad faces or tick and cross for like/dislike. Count how many children like each type of egg. What type do children like the most/least? If one more child liked scrambled egg how many like it now? Look at other ways to collect the information, for example children sorting themselves into groups showing their favourite type.

Birthday celebrations

Cooking is naturally rich in mathematical learning opportunities. Children can explore measuring, shape, counting and time in purposeful contexts as they cook, bake and prepare food.

Explain that the children are in charge of catering for a birthday party for 10 children/toys and of setting the table for the party. Encourage them to make their own lists of what they will need to prepare the table, supporting the development of mathematical marks. The children are to collect the correct number of cups, plates and cutlery. Can they sort these ready to set the table for the party? Support the children in making place mats by drawing round a set of cutlery, plate and cup. Let the children create their own place mats and then set the table by matching each item to the shape on the place mat. What would happen if 2 more children/toys wanted to join the party? What if 3 children/toys couldn't come? Talk about the number of guests for the party. Can the children number the chairs so that each guest knows where to sit and so that they can check they have the correct amount?

Decorating biscuits

Have a selection of bought or made biscuits of different shapes and sizes. Can the children count the biscuits and talk about their shape and size? Are there enough biscuits for everyone to decorate 2 each? How could we find out? Children make the icing for the biscuits using measuring spoons or small cups of water and icing sugar to mix together. Count how many times the icing is mixed before it is ready. Talk about how many spoons of icing the children will need to ice their biscuit. Show the children a range of fruit or sweets to decorate their biscuits and discuss how many each child can have, such as 5. This could be done by leaving bowls of topping with a numeral by the tray of bowls for children to talk about why the number is there and recognise how many they can have. If someone has 3 can anyone help to tell them how many more they can take? How many different ways can you put these toppings on your 2 biscuits? Can they record this through drawings, writing of numerals or using simple number sentences? Compare their biscuits. Do they have the same amount of toppings? Does one have more/less? Have they chosen the same type of toppings as their friend?

Main activity 1

Healthy fruit smoothie
You will need:

- A range of familiar and exotic fruit
- Blender
- Blunt knives
- A measuring cup
- Drinking cups
- Large paper

Getting started

Explain that for snack time you would like to make a healthy snack using fruit. Show the children a range of fruit and ask for their ideas about what could be made. Discuss the idea of making fruit smoothies. Have they had one before? Look at the ingredients and equipment on the table and discuss how it could be made. Make a picture recipe with the children for making the fruit smoothie. Ask children to number the steps using mathematical marks and encourage the use of ordinals and language of time whilst completing the recipe, such as 'first', 'next', 'second'.

Main activity

Talk about how the fruit needs to be cut up before it is put into the blender/bowl. Use a selection of fruit for children to cut with blunt knives and talk about how many pieces they have cut the fruit into. Can they cut their banana/grapes into half? If we need 5 pieces of apple, how could we cut it up to have the correct amount? Discuss how to measure out the fruit juice to add to the fruit. When measuring the juice using a measuring cup, talk about whether the cup is 'full', 'half full' or 'nearly full' each time. Children to measure out cups of fruit juice and put them into the blender/bowl with the fruit until the children/adult decide there is enough. Blend the fruit and fruit juice and count how many seconds it needs until it is smooth. Ask the children if they think there is enough smoothie for everyone in the group. How could we make sure that everyone has the same amount? Could we mark the cups so that each cup has the same amount in? Talk about how full the cups are and count how many empty cups are left.

What next?

- During snack time, ask children to complete a like/dislike chart for the fruit smoothie. Children to write their names or draw a picture of themselves under a smiley or sad face to show whether they liked it or not.

- Leave the picture recipe that was made with the children with a selection of fruit for them to make their own smoothies, by cutting the fruit into the correct number of pieces and measuring juice using cups. (An adult will need to blend the smoothie when the children are finished.)

- After cooking other snack items or food at home, can children draw or make their own photo recipes to describe to others using mathematical language?

Main activity 2

Going shopping

You will need:

- A range of tins and packets of food from supermarkets
- Card for price tags
- Sticky labels
- Shopping bags or baskets
- A till
- Pretend or real money

Getting started

Play the memory game of 'I went to the supermarket and I bought . . .'. Can they remember what was bought first, second, last? Explain that they are going to set up a supermarket using tins and packets that you have provided. Discuss how to set up a shop and talk about issues such as 'How will people know how much each item is?', 'What will we need to buy the items?', 'Who works in a shop and what do they need?'

Main activity

Provide the children with the supermarket items and some sticky labels or card shaped as price tags. Show the children real or pretend pennies and talk about how to pay for items, for example using two pennies for something that costs two pence. Can they make small amounts, initially up to 5p, then 10p and beyond? Talk about the prices that could be put on each item and ask the children to label each packet or tin with a sticky label or price tag. Observe how they represent their prices, for example by writing numerals, making marks or drawing round pennies or spots. Allow children time to set up the shop by pricing the items, organising them and sorting coins for the till. Explain that every child will have 5 pennies. They can visit the supermarket with a basket or bag and buy one item. Can they count out the correct number of pennies to pay for their item? The checkout assistant has the role of checking the money and collecting the money in the till. What if they now have more pennies and buy more than one item? How could they work out how many pennies they will need altogether to pay for their items? Provide some small pads or paper for the children to make their own shopping lists for what they are going to buy and the price it will cost. How will they record this? Could they draw around the correct number of pennies they need to pay for the items exactly?

What next?

- Give the children 10p and ask them to find out how many items they could buy for their money.
- Tell the children that all the items in the shop are now 1p more expensive. Can they make new price tags for the items with the new prices? This could also be repeated for a 1p discount.

Look, listen and note

- Are they using their developing ideas to solve problems in the context?
- What strategies are the children using to match quantities with numbers?
- How do children count an irregular arrangement of up to ten objects?
- How do children find the sum of two numbers or quantities?
- What language do the children use when they compare, sort or order objects or quantities?

? Key questions

- How can you find out . . .?
- What is the same/different about these objects/quantities?
- How many are there altogether?
- Is there the same amount/more/less?
- How can we show what we have found out?

Key vocabulary

Counting: Number, zero, one, two, three up to ten, how many? Count, many, few, guess how many, estimate, nearly, first, second, third...tenth

Calculating: Add, more, less, and, make, total, altogether, take (away), leave

Solving problems: Sort, order, same, different, find, choose, collect, use, make, tell me, describe, talk about, instructions, explain, half, halve, colour, tick, cross, draw, ring

Measures: Measure, size, compare, enough, not enough, too much, too little, nearly, full, half full, empty, holds, container, weigh, weighs, balances, heavy/light, heavier/lighter, heaviest/lightest, balance, scales, weight

Pattern: Size, bigger, larger, smaller, pattern, repeating pattern, match

Using money: Count out, share out, left, left over, total, money, coin, penny, pence, pound, price, cost, buy, sell, spend, spent, pay, change, costs more, cheap, costs less, costs the same as, how much . . .? How many . . .?

Health and safety

- Ensure children are supervised when using any sharp cooking implements.
- Ensure adults handle equipment such as the blender.
- Ensure safety precautions are followed when using an oven or hob so that children are unable to touch or be close to these appliances by zoning off the cooking area and that adults handle all hot equipment and leave food to cool in a safe area.
- Remind children about not putting anything in their mouths unless they have been told it is safe to eat.
- Ensure all adults are aware of any food allergies or cultural/religious restrictions on food and eating before doing any cooking activities.

Useful stories and rhymes

Oranges and lemons

Sing a song of sixpence

Hot cross buns

The Queen of Hearts
These traditional rhymes are useful starting points for cooking activities.

5 currant buns in a baker's shop (Traditional rhyme)
This counting song is an ideal way in for learning about money and one less. It would be useful to practise before undertaking the 'Going shopping' activity to ensure children are familiar with pennies.

Hansel and Gretel (Traditional tale)
A traditional tale which is a lovely way in for talking about food and preferences children have, linked to sweet treats.

The enormous turnip (Traditional tale)
A repetitive story to help children understand where our food comes from. This is a good starting point for 'printing patterns' using vegetables, including turnips.

Links to theory

Research into the role parents and families play in the education of children is widespread. All practitioners know how important it is that concepts being explored in educational settings are supported at home by parents. *The Impact of Parental Involvement on Children's Education* (DfES 2003) outlines the pivotal role parents play as children's first educators. It states that the involvement of parents in their child's education can have a significant impact on their success and achievement, as researched in *The Impact of Parental Involvement, Parental Support and Family Education on Pupil Achievement and Adjustment* (Desforges, 2003). The provision of food and cookery is an ideal area to engage parents and encourage support at home.

What does this look like in practice?

Practitioners should endeavour to engage parents in all aspects of the curriculum. However, this particular area of provision provides opportunities for links with home to be made easily and effectively. Parents could be invited into the setting to share food with the children, to support cooking that is planned or to cook their own recipes with the children. By involving the parents in the setting, practitioners can model how mathematics is inherent within food and cooking so that this can continue to be supported at home. Ideas for supporting children at home can also be sent to parents, such as recipe ideas or activities linked to breakfast or dinner time to develop mathematical concepts. It is also vital for practitioners to highlight to parents that support should be given in real-life situations such as shopping at the supermarket, cooking breakfast or setting the table for meals.

Making mathematical marks

- Making price tags for shopping items or signs for the supermarket
- Recording likes and dislikes showing the most popular choice
- Recording by drawing coins to show prices or money to go shopping
- Recording their outcomes through drawings, writing numerals or using simple number sentences
- Recording the recipe for making smoothies and ordering instructions using marks, numerals or language of time

9 | Music making and sounds

Why music making and sounds are important

There is an inherent link between maths and music, based on recognising and creating meaning in patterns, within both sound and numbers. A strong sense of rhythm and pattern in music will therefore support mathematical learning. This chapter will look at the use of instruments, bodies and voices to develop a sense of rhythm and pattern. Making instruments with children offers purposeful reasons for looking at capacity, measures and counting. Number rhymes are a wonderful way for children to start to learn about adding and subtracting.

Links to other areas of learning

Personal Social and Emotional Development	• Working cooperatively, and taking turns to make music • Maintaining attention and concentrating when listening to sounds, songs and music • Selecting and using a range of instruments independently to explore music making
Communication and Language	• Sustaining listening by using music or sounds • Enjoying listening to and participating in songs, music and rhymes, and making up their own based on these • Brainstorming music words to extend vocabulary, for example loud, quiet, pluck, beat, pulse
Literacy	• Writing or orally telling instructions for making and playing instruments • Making signs or captions to accompany a range of instruments

Understanding the World	• Finding out about music and instruments from other times and places • Listening to and talking about music and songs from different cultures and for a range of celebrations • Investigating objects using all of the senses by identifying different sounds made by a range of instruments and how those sounds are made • Using ICT music programs or electronic devices such as electric keyboards or guitars to explore different sounds • Listening to music related to seasons, events and festivals
Physical Development	• Handling tools and objects safely • Using tools to create an effect with materials to construct their own instrument • Singing songs or rhymes about being healthy, for example about fruit or vegetables for healthy eating
Expressive Arts and Design	• Selecting the tools and materials needed to make their own instruments • Using techniques to ensure instruments make a sound, such as stretching elastic bands, using split peas, etc • Expressing and communicating ideas, thoughts and feelings through the use of instruments and songs • Developing an understanding of how music can represent ideas, thoughts and emotions • Building a larger repertoire of songs and singing these from memory • Exploring changing and making sounds using percussion instruments or self-made instruments • Recognising sound patterns and repeated sounds • Using imagination in music making
Mathematics	• Measures – length, capacity • Counting and numbers • Ordinal numbers • Calculating • Sorting

Key resources

• A range of percussion instruments such as tambourines, drums, bells, cymbals, shakers

- Junk modelling resources, for example plastic cups, ice cream boxes, elastic bands, tissue paper, kitchen rolls
- Instrument picture cards
- Dried foods to fill instruments, such as split peas or rice
- Microphones
- Earphones
- CD player and a range of CDs of music or number songs and rhymes

Maths web

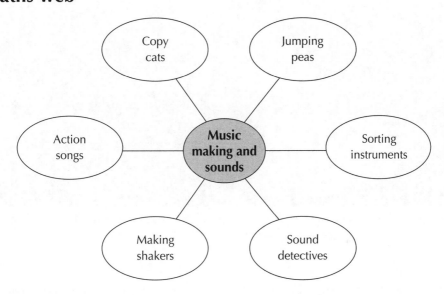

Jumping peas

Leave a range of drums of differing sizes out with rice or split peas. Set the children the challenge of putting the drums in order according to size. How will they do this? Can the children compare the drums by placing them next to each other or on top of each other? Practice counting the number of sounds they can hear as they explore playing them. Leave some number cards near the drums for the children to practise beating the drum the correct number of times to match the numeral on the card. Now explain that children can use the rice and split peas by putting some on top of the drums. Challenge the children to see who can beat the drums the most amount of times before the rice or peas fall off the top of the drum. How could they record their scores? Leave a large board for them to explore their ideas for scoring. Is there a difference between how many times they can beat the small drums compared to the larger ones?

Sorting instruments

Exploring musical instruments provides endless opportunities to learn about counting, matching, patterns, timing, shape and size.

Give the children various percussion instruments and a selection of boxes or baskets to sort the instruments. Can they talk about how they have sorted them? Play the instruments with the children and talk to them about the types of sounds they make. Can the children sort them according to their sound? Then compare another feature, such as size. Help the children to re-sort the instruments using other criteria. How could the baskets/boxes be labelled to show their sorting? Could children make drawings to show how they have sorted the instruments? Give the children picture labels for sorting circles and allow them time to sort, for example ones they can shake and ones that can't be shaken to make a noise.

Sound detectives

Blindfold the children in a small group and provide a range of percussion instruments in the centre of the circle. An adult plays a number of sounds on one instrument. The children have to count the sounds they hear and then remove the blindfolds. They then represent this number as a numeral or mark on paper to hold up, or select a numeral card to show how many sounds they heard. Who was right? Did anyone show a number that was too many or too few? Play the sounds again without the blindfold and talk about how to count the sounds they can see and hear the adult playing. What if one more/less sound was played, how many would it be this time? Check using the instruments. Allow children time to continue this game without an adult. Can they play sounds for the group to count and then check each other's ideas about the number of sounds they heard?

Making shakers

Look at a range of shakers and talk about what makes the sound when they are shaken. Do the children think the shaker is completely full? Would it make a sound if it was full? Give children a range of junk modelling resources such as plastic cups and yogurt pots to make shakers. Allow them time to choose the container they want to use. Talk about who they think has the container that holds the most/least. When making shakers, talk to the children about how much rice/split peas they will need and how they will measure these out. Give a selection of cups or spoons to explore how to fill the cup to 'half full', 'nearly full' or 'nearly empty'. Which shaker is the best? How full is it of rice? Do their own shakers have the same amount of rice, or more, or less? If the shaker needed to be half full, how many spoons of rice will we need to make the container half full? Which shaker would need the most spoons of rice to make it half full?

Action songs

Play children a range of familiar songs and allow them to explore making sequences of actions or movements to match the music. Can they copy or recreate a set of actions/ movements? How many times did you clap/pat your head? How many different actions can you link together? How many actions have we done altogether? What if we miss out the . . ., how many now? Next explore using sounds children make with their bodies such as clicking, clapping, tapping and stamping. Encourage them to make up some repeating sequences such as clap, clap, stamp. Can other children copy these patterns? What would come next after a stamp? Could they make this pattern now with four actions?

Copy cats

Children work in a group with an adult with a set of instruments. The adult plays a short sound pattern on an instrument and the children try to copy this pattern. Children then create their own sound patterns for others to copy. Ask the children to find out how many sounds they have played in each pattern. How could we record these patterns?

Do the number of marks we've made match the number of sounds we've played? Practise saying the number names as the sounds are played, to demonstrate how to count the sounds they hear. What is the greatest number of sounds they can play on their instruments? Provide a wider range of instruments for them to explore more sound making and pattern building.

Main activity 1

Royal instruments
You will need:

- A range of percussion instruments such as shakers, drums, triangles, guiros, tambourines, bells
- Large cards with a tick or a cross on
- Sorting circles
- Pens/pencils
- Large paper

Getting started

Sit children on the floor and give each an instrument. Explain that you are collecting instruments for a character, for example a princess or a king, who only likes certain instruments. Children explore the sounds that their instruments make. Talk about how sounds are made on each of the instruments, for example by being shaken, scraped or tapped. Count how many children have each type of percussion instrument.

Main activity

Remind children that the king/princess will only have certain instruments played in the castle. Can the children help to work out which type of instruments have been chosen? Children play their instruments one at a time and are told whether each instrument can be taken to the princess's or king's castle, possibly using large cards with a tick or a cross. Children then work out the criteria used to decide which instruments could be taken to the castle, for example by putting all of the instruments that are allowed to be taken to the castle in the middle of the circle to observe the similarities between them. Repeat this game so that children understand how to choose a criteria for the instruments, for example by the way they are played or the type of instrument, such as all the drums. Children then take on the role of choosing the criteria and tell each child whether an instrument can be taken to the castle using the tick and cross cards. Ask the children how we could record which instruments to take to the castle – provide them with paper and pencils and sorting rings. Support the sorting of the instruments and discuss the best way to record their findings.

What next?

- Provide a similar selection of instruments but in a range of sizes and colours to encourage children to explore alternative ways of sorting.
- The 'Sorting instruments' activity could follow this game, for children to attempt independent sorting of instruments using their own or given criteria.
- Play the children a range of instruments or music and talk about their favourite sounds/songs. Talk about how they could find out which is the most popular sound/song in the setting. Allow children time to investigate this, perhaps by asking their friends, and then model how to collect the information using sorting rings with pictures of the children or room for them to write their names in sorting rings on paper.

Main activity 2

Creating an orchestra
You will need:

- A range of percussion instruments, such as bells, tambourines, drums, guiros, maracas and shakers
- Instrument picture cards
- Sticky labels
- Card/paper to make number/spotted/marked cards

Getting started

Explain that the children are going to be part of a real orchestra and that they are going to take part in a performance. The children need to perform a piece of music and are each in charge of one instrument. Talk about how to ensure that the instruments are not all played at the same time and that it is important for each child to know how many times to beat/pluck/shake the instrument. Discuss how they will do this. Suggest the use of picture cards so that they only play an instrument when they see that instrument held up.

Main activity

Show the children the instrument picture cards and then talk about how to indicate how many times the children will play their instruments. Allow children time to discuss this and prepare some cards with numerals, marks or spots on to show how many times to play the instrument. Establish who will be playing 1st, 2nd, 3rd and so on by picking the instrument cards in order, for example shakers first, then drums, then bells. Children are to be in a circle or line in order with their instrument picture cards in front of them. Emphasise ordinal language when they are organising themselves. Make labels together to stick on the children to show the order of who is playing, for example a number 1, or using a dot/mark for first, on the labels. Have one child as a conductor holding up the number/spotted/marked cards to show each performer how many sounds they will make with their instrument. Practise the performance by allowing the conductor to choose number/spotted/marked cards for each instrument and performers to play the right number of sounds (the conductor's job is also to check they have played the correct number by counting the sounds). Once the children are able to play the correct number of sounds the orchestra can perform to other children. Can the audience guess which number the conductor was holding up if they are unable to see the cards?

What next?

- Challenge the current orchestra by asking questions such as, 'What if one more child wanted to join the orchestra, how many would we have now?', 'What if one child wants to leave?'

- Set up a small group of children who have been part of the audience with a box of instruments to create their own orchestra. Ask questions such as 'Are there enough instruments for every child to have one instrument?' or 'How many could they have each?' Observe how they solve these problems.

- Provide a greater selection of instruments and ask children to plan a new orchestra using drawings and mathematical labels, such as planning the number of children needed, who will be first, second, etc. Ask the children to record the number of instruments they have and the number of sounds they are going to play.

Look, listen and note

- Are children able to count sounds that they cannot see?
- How do children begin to represent numbers? Do they use marks, numerals, fingers or pictures?
- What observations do they make about patterns? Can they continue or copy a simple pattern?
- What language do they use to talk about capacity, number, counting and sorting?
- How do they record their ideas or thinking?

Key questions

- Can you tell me what would come next in this pattern?
- How many . . .?
- How can we count the sounds?
- How can we show our ideas about numbers on paper?
- What would happen if . . .?

Key vocabulary

Counting: Number, zero, one, two, three...ten, how many...? Count, many, few, guess how many, estimate, first, second, third...tenth

Calculating: Add, more, and, make, total, altogether, take (away), more, less, is the same as, how many fewer is... than...? How many more to make...? How many more is... than...?

Solving problems: Sort, order, same, different, find, choose, collect, use, make, tell me, describe, talk about, instructions, explain, tick, cross, draw, record, describe, carry on, continue, repeat, show me, listen, join in, remember, start from, start with, what comes next?

Measures: Measure, size, compare, enough, not enough, too much, too little, too many, too few, nearly, full, half full, empty, holds, container

Pattern: Size, bigger, larger, smaller, pattern, repeating pattern, match, copy

⊞ Health and safety

- Ensure children are supervised when filling their instruments using rice or split peas to ensure these are not put into their mouths.

- Use appropriate-sized instruments for young children which are safe to use with no small removable parts.

📖 Useful stories and rhymes

I am the music man (Traditional rhyme)
A well-known song which can introduce a range of instruments.

Head, shoulders, knees and toes (Traditional rhyme)
A familiar action song which can help to develop sequencing and copying actions before completing the 'copy cat' activity.

5 little speckled frogs

10 fat sausages

5 little men in a flying saucer

5 currant buns in a baker's shop

10 green bottles

5 little ducks

These traditional number rhymes and songs are an effective way of introducing and consolidating the concepts of addition, take away, more and less.

Links to theory

Shinichi Suzuki

Children will have explored and experienced a range of sounds since birth, making sense of important sounds in their world, such as recognising the noise of a train as 'choo choo' or the sound of their mother's voice.

Suzuki believed that children are not born with a musical talent but that this can be developed through rich, varied opportunities in both the home and the education setting. He stated that this concept is true of all areas of learning; however, in the creative arts such as music parents or practitioners often believe that children either do or do not have the innate talent to succeed (Cooney, Cross and Trunk 1993).

What does this look like in practice?

Practitioners should embrace the ideas of Suzuki in their settings, believing that modelling and frequent opportunities to explore music and sound can lead to children being successful and excited musicians. There should be a range of provision in this area such as musical instruments for children to listen to and explore playing, a varied selection of music, including a range of genres and composers/singers and opportunities to create their own instruments. Through repetition of sounds, rhythms, pitch and tempo children will begin to understand and explore the patterns within music which will support their understanding and awareness of patterns within mathematics.

Making mathematical marks

- Creating number/spotted cards by making marks on paper
- Recording their sorting of instruments, for example drawing sorting circles, using pictures, ticks/crosses or marks to show their thinking
- Making marks to match the number of sounds being played on instruments
- Leaving large paper or a board for children to record marks or numerals for their scores
- Using marks, shapes or tallies for recording sounds being played by instruments

10 | ICT

Why ICT is important

Today's world is full of technology and children are becoming increasingly familiar with equipment such as digital cameras, mobile phones and computers. They also encounter ICT in their everyday lives: tills at the supermarket, barcodes and scanners, digital clocks on appliances, calculators and remote controls. Televisions now have many channels and as a result even the youngest children can tell you which three digits they need to input for their favourite channels, using remote controls to find these. ICT links naturally to mathematics in the early years and provides opportunities for children to learn skills which they will continue to develop throughout their lives. The most common piece of ICT equipment children encounter is a computer, but for the purposes of this chapter we have focused on other types of ICT appliances, as by and large Early Years software tends to be self-explanatory and specific in its nature. It is vital to expand our notion of ICT beyond the computer alone and to encourage children to access and learn to use and control a whole range of ICT equipment.

Links to other areas of learning

Personal Social and Emotional Development	• Developing the ability to cooperate with others when using equipment such as walkie talkies, microphones or cameras
	• Using cameras to photograph children to show a range of emotions, and then using the photos as a stimulus for discussion or circle time

Communication and Language	• Talking books played through CD players or Interactive Whiteboards
	• Using microphones and CD or tape players to record stories, ideas or rhymes
	• Exploring electronic books with sounds that accompany the stories
	• Using CDs or Internet sites to play stories, songs or music to develop children's listening and concentration skills
Literacy	• Using simple word processing programs to record names, captions or ideas
	• Developing reading skills by recognising and using icons and images to cause something to happen such as when clicking on hyperlinks
Understanding the World	• Investigating the use of technology in our world, such as the use of barcode scanners in supermarkets and libraries
	• Programming simple devices such as floor turtles to move along a route or from one place to another
	• Using the Internet to find out about the world around us or to answer questions
Physical Development	• Using the mouse on the computer to develop motor skills and hand–eye coordination.
	• Exploring giving instructions through movement in the outdoor area or large inside space before programming simple devices
Expressive Arts and Design	• Using simple paint programs to create pictures or images to represent ideas
	• Using video cameras to record children's performances linked to dance or role play
	• Developing composition skills using simple music programs to create pieces of music by combining sounds
	• Developing children's appreciation of a range of music through the use of CDs; talking about the music, instruments and feelings the music invokes
	• Using microphones for singing through role play or for performances
Mathematics	• Counting
	• Number
	• Calculating
	• Time
	• Solving Problems
	• Direction
	• Position

Key resources

- Walkie talkies
- Microphones (to record sounds and for role play)
- Tape and CD players
- Computer
- Old laptops
- Telephones
- Programmable toys
- Remote control toys
- Cameras (for role play) and digital cameras

Maths web

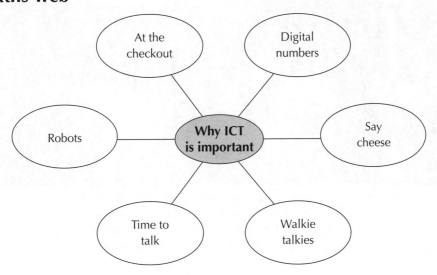

Digital numbers

Collect together a range of different clocks including both analogue and digital. Talk to the children about them. How do they look the same? How do they look different? Where have they seen clocks before? Why do we need clocks? Write a number for the children to see as it would appear on an analogue and then also a digital clock. Stress that it is the same number but just looks different. Explore other digital numbers with the children and talk about how they are made up of small lines. Provide the children with lolly sticks, drinking straws, sticks and twigs and encourage them to have a go at making their own digital numbers. Make sure you have some large ones on display for them to refer to. Their numbers can be stuck onto paper to make pictures, or alternatively sticks from their numbers can be taken and moved to form different numbers. Older children can investigate how many sticks they need to make each number and which numbers need the most/fewest sticks.

Say cheese

Simple cameras provide a great way for children to record instantly their mathematical discoveries, whether in the form of shapes, numbers and patterns spotted in the environment or in models, pictures and patterns they have made themselves. Children can reflect on these photographs and assess their own learning.

Digital cameras are becoming cheaper to purchase and there is no need to buy a 'childproof' rubber-covered camera for children. Make sure that the camera you purchase is easy to use and spend time showing the children how to use it and look after it. Tell the children that you are getting a bit forgetful and can't remember how to do things. Ask them to help you take some photographs to remind you. Choose a familiar activity or daily routine to focus on and encourage the children to take photos at each stage, for example getting ready to go outside, making playdough or setting up the snack table. Print the photographs out and sit with the children putting them into the correct order. Encourage use of sequential language such as first, next, after, then, before, finally and so on. Encourage the children to record their own captions to go with the pictures and display these for them to refer to.

Walkie talkies

Walkie talkies are great for helping to develop speaking and listening as children have to rely upon these skills when using them. Children work in pairs. One child hides something in the garden and takes a seat at the other end; the other has to try to find the hidden object, by following instructions given by the partner over the walkie talkie. Encourage children to use everyday positional and directional language such as forwards, back, next to, in front of, under and over. Once the child has found the hidden objects the children swap over. This could be extended by hiding more than one object, creating a trail to follow.

Time to talk

Show the children a range of phones, including land line phones and mobiles. Most phones now have keypads, so children would probably enjoy exploring an old-fashioned one with a dial. Look at the phones together. What buttons can they see? Can they see any numbers or symbols? Challenge them to press a number you call out, initially just one number, gradually increasing to a series of numbers. Look at some phone books together and tell the children that they are going to make their own phone books. Children can draw pictures of themselves or their friends (or use photos) and then record their own attempts at numerals next to these. These could be laminated and used for play. Provide children with a range of small cardboard boxes and tell them they are going to make their own phones. Provide squares of paper to be the keys and encourage the children to stick these on and record their own marks on them; provide real phones for them to refer to. Once these are made, keep them as a role play resource along with the phone books the children made.

Robots

Explore large movements in the outdoor area and tell the children that they are going to be robots that have to follow your commands. This can be made more exciting by preparing some boxes covered in foil for robot heads! Give some simple instructions using a robot voice, for example taking a certain number of steps forward. Start by just giving them one instruction, and then gradually increase this to include a series of 2, 3 or more instructions. Invite children to have a go at being in charge and giving instructions. Try to include positional and directional language such as forwards, backwards, sideways, turn, go over, straight ahead, under, next to, around, over and so on. Once children are familiar with these types of simple instructions, introduce some programmable toys and explain that these are also robots. Can the children make them do the same types of things? Can they find ways of recording their instructions or the different paths the robots took?

At the checkout

If possible, arrange a visit to a local supermarket before this activity so that children can see a real checkout in action. Collect together a range of items to show the children, including products such as books, food, CDs, DVDs and anything else you can find with a barcode. Also include some loose fruit and vegetables that do not have a barcode. Give the children items to look at and ask them if they know which part the checkout person would put over the scanner. Using a pretend checkout till, ask the children to show you what the checkout person would do with the items. Talk about the barcode. What does it look like? What can they see? Talk about the lines. Are they all the same length and thickness? Talk about how the till has a computer in it that recognises the barcode and then knows what the item is. Discuss how this helps shops know what they need to get more of. Ask the children to look at the numbers. Can they see any they recognise? Provide some rectangular pieces of white paper, some black pens or paint and different-sized brushes. Challenge the children to make their own barcodes using thick and thin lines, with numerals along the bottom. These could be displayed along with some real boxes with bar codes on them. This could be developed further through the provision of a shop role play area with a checkout, scanner and lots of real items to scan.

Main activity 1

Remote control toys

You will need:

- A collection of working remote control toys
- Mark making materials
- Large wooden blocks

Getting started

Check all the toys are working before starting the activity. Start by arranging the remote control toys together in a group and put the remote controls in a separate group.

Main activity

When the children enter the setting, show them the remote control toys and explain that they have been left in a muddle. How can we find out which remote control controls each toy? Listen to and record the children's ideas. Can they predict which control will make each toy work? Look at the remote controls to see if they have any similarities to the toys. Do they give you any clues as to which toy they control? Let the children explore the controls and investigate what happens. Can they match the controls to the toys? Ensure that the children have time to play freely with the toys before developing the activity further, talking about the direction they are taking.

Explain to the children that the toys need something to do and suggest building a park or playground for them. Provide a range of construction materials such as wooden blocks, cardboard boxes and other items for them to use. Challenge the children to build structures for the toys to travel under, around, between, over and through. Once the children have built their playground area for the toys, encourage them to take turns to direct their toys through the course. This could be extended by adding the use of timers to record the time taken for toys to proceed through the park or playground. Talk about where the toys are going, promoting positional and directional language.

What next?

- Provide clipboards, whiteboards or paper for children to record their park or playground on, encouraging them to record the journeys their toys took.
- Timers could be used to measure the time taken by various toys to complete the course and times could be recorded on a flipchart. This could lead to discussions about which toy was the fastest/slowest. Medals could be made for 1st, 2nd and 3rd place. Do bigger toys go faster? Do smaller toys go slower?
- Provide large pieces of paper for children to make maps for the toys to travel on, with arrows, signs and symbols
- Attach a number to each of the structures and challenge the children to navigate the toys to each one in the correct order.

Main activity 2

The music studio
You will need:

- Musical instruments
- A quiet area away from the rest of the setting
- Tape recorder and blank tapes Microphones
- A range of books and posters featuring number songs and rhymes

Getting started

Set up the area as a music studio with instruments, number rhyme books and posters. Provide some blank tapes and a tape recorder with microphones if the recorder does not have a built-in one.

Main activity

Show the children the area. What do they think they could do there? Show them the pictures of number rhymes and the books. Do they recognise any of these rhymes? Explain to the children that they will be pop stars for the day and you would like them to make a tape for the whole group to listen to of number rhymes. Which rhymes would they like to perform? Let the children choose some instruments and practise singing and playing some of their favourite number rhymes. Show the children how to record onto the blank tape. Use a drum to beat 3, 4 or 5 beats to count them in for each song; children can take on this role and the number of beats can be varied according to the age and experience of the children. Encourage them to play their instruments and sing the songs together. Ensure that different groups of children have the opportunity to record songs and perhaps involve some parents and carers, including those who can record some number songs in other languages. Once the children have recorded a few songs, listen to the tape as a whole group and then join in by singing and playing along. Talk to the children about which was their favourite song. Make a simple tally chart to illustrate their favourite songs.

What next?

- Extend the activity by asking children to play an instrument the correct number of times between each verse, indicating how many are left, for example 8 bangs on the drum after the second person falls out of the bed, or 4 shakes of the bells after the first frog jumped into the pool.

- Develop a karaoke area, where children sing along to number rhymes and play along to CDs.

- Challenge the children to create and record sound patterns using the instruments and find ways of recording these on paper using signs, symbols and numbers. Share these with the group, pausing the tape after each one and challenging children to copy them.

Look, listen and note

- Are children using their developing ideas to solve problems in practical contexts?

- Observe children's understanding and use of positional and directional language, such as on top, under, behind, next to, between, forwards, backwards, sideways and so on.

- How are children developing their counting skills and attempting to record numerals?

- Do children enjoy joining in with number rhymes? Can they use developing methods to solve the related simple calculations (1 more, 1 less)?

Key questions

- How are these things the same? How are they different?
- Can you tell me about the path you took?
- What do you think will happen next?
- Can you find a way to make this work?
- How can we record what you have done to help us another day?

Key vocabulary

Counting: Count, 1, 2, 3 up to 10 and beyond, same, different, first, second, third and so on

Calculating: More, less, altogether, one more, two more, take away, one less, two less

Time: How long, minutes, timer, clock, first, next, after, before

Position: Over, under, above, below, top, bottom, side, on, in, around, in front, behind, front, back

Direction: Left, right, up, down, forwards, backwards, sideways, across, close, far

Health and safety

- Practitioners need to ensure that electrical toys are checked regularly to see that they are still in good working order. Batteries must be checked and replaced regularly to reduce the risk of leakage.
- Staff need to make children aware of the dangers of electricity and supervise children when they are using electrical equipment, ensuring any unused sockets are fitted with socket covers.
- Practitioners need to ensure that any software used has educational value and is age appropriate.
- Children should always be supervised when using the computer even when security programs are in place, and especially when accessing the Internet.

Useful stories and rhymes

What's the Time Mr Wolf? (Colin Hawkins, Mammoth, 1983)

Hickory dickory dock (Traditional rhyme)
These both link to clocks and telling the time and could be adapted to include digital times.

You're All Animals (Nicholas Allan, Red Fox, 2001)
Links to sending emails and using the computer.

Harry and the Robots (Ian Whybrow and Adrian Reynolds, Puffin, 2000)
Offers opportunities to explore shape, pattern, colour and numbers. Links well to robots and model making activities.

Let's Go Shopping (Keep Me Busy) (Dawn Sirett, Dorling Kindersley, 2006)
Links to using money, shopping, shapes, weighing, sorting and paying using a chip and pin machine.

Links to theory

Carole Aubrey and Sarah Dahl

Aubrey and Dahl in *A Review of the Evidence on the Use of ICT in the Early Years Foundation Stage* (2008) drew together a whole range of international evidence and research around ICT in the Early Years. They viewed ICT as all-encompassing and extending far beyond the computer, incorporating everyday equipment that supports and develops learning (and real-life skills) for young children. Aubrey and Dahl identified how ICT can play an important role in young children's all-round development, but included a particular reference to problem solving skills (p. 38). They also considered the ICT experience children bring from home and how this can greatly vary, sometimes because of socio-economic factors. Aubrey and Dahl stressed that practitioners need to work with parents and develop ways to support those children with low levels of experiences to ensure equal opportunities.

What does this look like in practice?

ICT extends far beyond the computer and completing educational games, although these do have value and some useful Early Years maths titles are available. Children must have opportunities to access a whole range of ICT resources within the setting to support their learning in all areas. ICT is an area of provision where resources can be limited, and practitioners need to ensure children have equal opportunities to access activities and plan effectively for this. Practitioners also need to model the correct, careful and safe use of equipment such as cameras and CD players, whilst ensuring that children do have opportunities to explore and investigate everyday uses of ICT freely through play.

Making mathematical marks

- Provide opportunities to make digital numbers from a range of materials including paints, chalks, pens and crayons as well as sticks, twigs and strips of paper.
- Encourage children to record maps and plans of routes and journeys taken by robots and remote control toys.
- Provide resources for children to write captions to accompany photographs they have taken.

11 | **Out and about**

Why learning outside is important

This chapter focuses on the huge potential the outdoor environment offers as a vehicle for early mathematical learning. Learning outside in the Early Years does not just mean playing in the designated space directly outside a setting, but can also include trips to parks, woodlands, beaches and other local areas. These types of excursions are especially important where there is very little or no outside area available. When children experience mathematics outdoors, their senses are stimulated by the natural world and the resources within it. They are able to work on very large scales, making maths increasingly physical and sensory, and even messy. These are all aspects of mathematics that would be difficult and impractical to provide inside. The outdoor environment is inherently full of numbers, shapes and patterns both natural and man made for children to explore, discuss and ask questions about.

Links to other areas of learning

Personal Social and Emotional Development	• Developing social skills as children share, negotiate, take turns and work together
	• Building confidence as children take risks and face challenges
	• Helping children to develop independence as they access and select resources
	• Providing engaging play where children remain focused and persevere for long periods of time
	• Helping children to learn about behavioural boundaries, danger and keeping safe

Communication and Language	• Encouraging use of language, both real and imaginary • Stimulating curiosity, encouraging children to comment and ask questions about what they experience • Promoting listening skills as children tune in to the sounds within the environment
Literacy	• Providing numerous opportunities to mark make on small and large scales with man-made and natural resources • Offering an exciting environment for role play and small world play; exploring settings, characters, sequence of events and plot within stories • Developing reading skills as children read labels and signs in the environment
Understanding the World	• Stimulating children's curiosity and interest in the natural environment • Encouraging children to observe and comment upon similarities and differences between objects, materials, living things and features of the environment • Helping children to learn about growth and change over time • Providing first-hand sensory experiences of the changing seasons and weather
Physical Development	• Enabling children to move freely in a variety of ways, developing spatial awareness • Developing coordination in small- and large-scale movements • Encouraging children to contribute to their health and wellbeing, helping them to learn about the importance of healthy lifestyles and choices • Helping children to learn about playing safely, transporting equipment and working with tools
Expressive Arts and Design	• Encouraging children to respond to what they experience • Providing opportunities for children to express and share their ideas, thoughts and feelings • Enabling children to be creative, on large and small scales, through role play, dance, art and design, and music • Stimulating imagination and creative thinking
Mathematics	• Counting • Shape and space • Number • Position • Calculation • Direction • Pattern • Measuring

Key resources

- Gardening tools (real child-sized tools, not plastic ones where possible)
- Water (ideally via a tap or hose or in large trays)
- Sand pit or tray (ideally big enough and deep enough to sit in)
- Digging area
- Decorators' paint brushes
- Large rolls of paper (wallpaper is ideal)
- Masking tape
- Large cardboard boxes
- Small baskets/bags for collecting objects
- Mark making materials
- Tyres and hoops
- Balls
- Buckets
- Natural resources such as logs, sticks, twigs, leaves, conkers, acorns, shells, pebbles, stones and mud
- Digital camera

Maths web

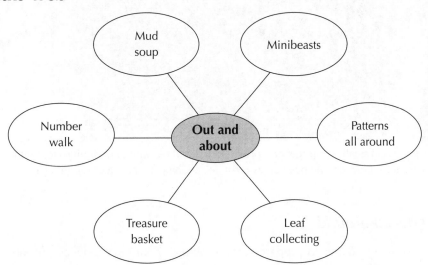

Minibeasts

Depending on the type of outdoor space you have, you could either focus on real minibeasts for this activity or hide some models of minibeasts around the area. Tell the children that they will be minibeast hunters for the day. Ask them where they think they might find minibeasts, modelling and encouraging the correct use of directional and positional language such as: 'under the log' or 'behind the tree'. Give children clipboards and pencils and challenge them to record the minibeasts they find. How many do they think they will find? Use minibeasts as a starting point to discuss similarities and differences. This could lead to some simple data handling by sorting according to types of minibeasts found.

This log-based small world scenario provides rich and relevant opportunities for children to explore direction and position as creatures are hidden and squeezed into spaces.

Patterns all around

Use crayons and paper to prepare some rubbings of various surfaces outside. Show these to the children and talk about what the patterns look like. Give the children the rubbings to take with them around the garden and challenge them to find where they think these came from. Provide paper and crayons and show the children how to make their own rubbings. If possible, take photographs of the areas they have made rubbings of. The photos and rubbings could then be used inside the setting for a display and discussions about patterns, shapes, similarities and differences.

Leaf collecting

Look at a sample of different leaves with the children and model and encourage the use of everyday language to describe their shape and size such as: pointy, curved, flat, big, small, tiny and so on. Tell the children that you will choose a leaf, and describe it, and they have to work out which one you are talking about. Provide small bags or baskets and send the children off around the area to find leaves. Depending on the age of the children this could be simply choosing their own leaves or made more challenging by providing them with set criteria recorded on small cards; for example, they must only find leaves of a certain colour or bigger than this leaf, smaller than this leaf, pointy leaves, round leaves and so on. Once the children have collected their leaves, look at them together and discuss them. Leaves could be matched, sorted by shapes, size or colour, or, where criteria cards have been given, children could look at the leaves collected by others and guess what their criteria might have been.

Treasure basket

Prepare some simple pictorial lists of objects for children to find outdoors such as leaves, sticks, daisies, blades of grass and stones. The lists could simply consist of pictures, but could also include a number to indicate how many of each thing needs to be found. Tell the children that they will be going on a treasure hunt and give each child a list as well as a basket or small bag for collecting items. This activity also works well in pairs, as one child can hold the list, marking off what is found, whilst the other holds the basket/bag. A timer could be used to make the challenge more exciting. Send the children off to find their treasure. Ask each child/pair to tell everyone else what they found or didn't find. What was the biggest/smallest/lightest/heaviest thing they found? How many things did they find altogether? Children could then go on to make their own treasure lists using pictures and numbers.

Number walk

Talk to the children about numbers. Where do they see numbers? Are there any numbers in their homes? Talk about numbers they might see on their way to school. Record these ideas, annotated with children's own words and use these as a basis for a display in the setting. Tell the children that you will be going on a number walk outside and provide them with magnifying glasses, binoculars (great when made from 2 kitchen roll tubes), clipboards and pencils and also take a digital camera. Go for a walk outside together and be on the lookout for numbers! As soon as anyone sees a number, make a big fuss, take a picture and encourage the children to have a go at recording it on their clipboard. Do any of them know what the number is? Why is it there? Is it telling us something? Continue with your walk, stopping and looking at numbers, encouraging the children to spot them and talk about them. On your return to the setting, talk about what you saw. Display the children's own mark making alongside photographs, drawings and the ideas you recorded before the walk. Involve parents by asking them to send in any photos or pictures of any other numbers the children see when they are out and about.

Mud soup

Set up a range of cooking utensils such as spoons, pots, pans, scales, jugs (real, not plastic toy ones, where possible) outside near the digging area, to be a bugs' kitchen. If at all possible set the area up near an outside tap so that the children can measure and collect their own water. Prepare a letter for the children from the bugs in the garden that are having a party and need some food made. Tell the children that the bugs have set up a special bug kitchen outside for the children to prepare the meals in, and have even left some recipes for them to follow. Find out what food they think the bugs might like. Children could explore the bug kitchen area freely, making their own concoctions, or could use simple prepared pictorial recipe cards to make soups, drinks and pies. These recipes could promote simple measuring by illustrating a numeral (how many/much) next to a picture of a measure (cups, spoons or spadefuls, bucket) next to the required ingredient (mud, grass, water, stones). Children could also make up their own recipe cards. Leave the 'food' out for the bugs overnight and prepare a thank you letter from the bugs for the next day, when the children return and the plates, pots and pans are mysteriously empty!

Main activity 1

Assault course
You will need:

- Large equipment such as tyres, hoops, benches, crates, boxes, cones, tunnels
- Clipboards, paper and pencils/pens
- Digital camera
- Timers such as stopwatches and sand timers

Outdoor spaces rich in interesting low-cost and no-cost resources motivate young children to explore shape, space and measures with their whole bodies.

Getting started

Talk to the children and ask them if they know what an assault course is. Have they ever had a go at one before? What sorts of things did they do? Model and encourage use of positional and sequential language: first, next, then, after, etc.

Main activity

Provide a range of equipment for children to use to develop their own assault courses. Which things do they want to use? What's going to be at the beginning and end of their course? Can they find something that their friends could climb over? Under? Go in between? Through? Go round? Encourage children to move equipment themselves safely, encouraging them to talk about how heavy things feel as they move them and the easiest and safest ways of transporting equipment (e.g. rolling tyres and hoops). What will the children have to do first in the assault course? Second? Third? Once the children have built their assault course, ask them to check whether there are things to go over, under, through, around, in between. Encourage children to have a go at the assault course, and join in with the others to chant 'over, over, over, over', 'under, under, under, under', 'around, around, around, around' as their friends complete the various sections.

Introduce the use of a stopwatch and show children how to use this. Allow the children some time to practise using the stopwatch to measure the time taken to complete the course. This could lead to a group competition, where children's names and times are recorded on a flipchart, leading to discussions about how long it took and who was the quickest. Children could then make medals for each other, celebrating their achievements on the course.

What next?

- Children could video each other and then watch the clip, commentating on what happened using positional, directional and sequential language.
- Provide large pieces of paper next to the assault course with marker pens and encourage children to try to make their own maps of the course, using arrows and other marks to show different pathways and routes.
- Let the children take photos of the various sections of the race. Use them to make different assault courses by putting them into different orders. Encourage them to set up the equipment to match the order of the pictures.

Main activity 2

Give it some welly!
You will need:

- Wellies
- Large paper (ideally wallpaper)
- Masking tape
- Various coloured paints in trays
- Clothes pegs

Getting started

Many settings now expect parents to provide a pair of wellies for their child to wear outside, making them a great 'real' resource for developing early problem solving skills. Use the children's wellies for these activities and if possible also include some very large and very small pairs too.

Before the children come into the setting, make various welly prints on a large piece of paper (wallpaper is ideal, fixed to the ground) using different boots and brightly coloured paint. Leave the track in the middle of the area surrounded by various wellies (including the ones used.)

Main activity

Leave the resources set up as above and, as the children see them, ask them what they think has happened. Suggest that perhaps the welly monster has been having a party with their wellies. Encourage the children to choose a welly to look at. Can they see anyone holding the matching one? Challenge the children to match wellies to welly prints. What type of print would their welly make? How would they describe the pattern on the sole? Has it got any numbers on it? Do they know what these numbers mean and why they are important? Let the children try to match wellies to prints and encourage talk about similarities and differences. Do they think anyone else's welly would make the same print? Provide more paper fixed securely to the floor and various wellies. Challenge the children to find wellies that fit them. Let the children stand in a tray of paint and make prints along the paper, exploring different shapes and pathways.

What next?

- Muddle all the wellies in a pile before the children come in and find out their ideas for sorting them. Provide clothes pegs for them to secure wellies into pairs.

- Find out the children's ideas about what they think the Welly Monster might look like. Work with them to make a large picture of the monster with lots of feet for wellies! Explain to the children that he likes all sorts of wellies but always likes to wear ones that have something the same about them. Prepare some laminated speech bubbles saying 'I like . . . wellies'. Use a whiteboard marker to add a word/picture/colour to the blank gap such as 'alien', 'green' or 'size 10'. Can the children choose the correct wellies from the pile to make the monster happy (matching the criteria) and match one to each of his feet? How many does he have? How many more does he need?

- Use the wellies in a shoe shop role play area. Explore arranging wellies in different ways such as according to height, sorting by colour or according to size. Take on the role of a customer looking for a certain type of welly. Can the children find any pairs you might like?

Look, listen and note

- Do children use the language of numbers and counting spontaneously as they explore the outdoor area?
- Are they able to count objects reliably, including when things are in irregular arrangements?
- Do children display an interest in solving problems?
- Can they describe journeys and routes using everyday language?
- Can children talk about similarities and differences between objects?
- Do they talk about shapes and patterns in the environment?

? Key questions

- Can you find something that looks the same as this one?
- Can you find something as big as your hand/as long as this stick/as small as this pebble?
- Can you tell me about the shapes/patterns you have made/can see?
- What's the same/different about these things?
- How could you record what you have done today?

Key vocabulary

Counting: Number, zero, one, two, three… to ten/twenty/beyond, how many…? count, more, less, first, second, third…

Calculating: Add, more, and, make, altogether, take away

Size: Big, small, long, short, high, low

Shape: (3D) cube, pyramid, sphere, cone; (2D) circle, triangle, square, rectangle, star, oval

Pattern: Repeating pattern, match, sort, same, different.

Position: Over, under, above, below, top, bottom, side, on, in, outside, inside, around, in front, behind, front, back

Direction: Left, right, up, down, forwards, backwards, sideways, across, close, far, near, along, through

⊞ Health and safety

- Children need to be reminded not to put any small objects into their mouths.
- Ensure there are no toxic plants within the area and remind children not to eat plants.
- Children should wash their hands thoroughly after working outside and especially before eating food.
- Be aware of any allergies such as reactions to bee stings or hay fever and the required treatment.

📖 Useful stories and rhymes

Mary, Mary quite contrary (Traditional rhyme)
Links to counting, sorting, shapes and patterns

The King of Tiny Things (Jeanne Willis, Puffin, 2010)
Offers opportunities for children to explore size and measuring.

It's the Bear! (Jez Alborough, Walker Books, 2004)

Where's My Teddy? (Jez Alborough, Walker Books, 2004)
Links to size, measuring, position and direction.

Leaf Man (Lois Elhert, Harcourt Children's Books, 2005)
Explores shape, patterns and pictures using natural objects.

Shark in the Dark (Nick Sharatt, David Fickling Books, 2010)

Shark in the Park (Nick Sharatt, Corgi Books, 2007)
Provide opportunities for children to explore shapes in the environment. Children can make their own kitchen roll tube telescopes.

Links to theory

Frederick Froebel

Froebel was an advocate of child-led learning and it was his work that led to the development of kindergartens (children's gardens). The notion of a learning environment as a place where children (plants) are nurtured by practitioners (gardeners) was central to his work. Froebel saw play as the natural way in which children learn about the world around them (Sutherland 1988). In terms of outdoor learning, kindergartens inspired by Froebel's work promote outdoor natural play, encouraging children to play and learn out of doors, enjoying and learning about nature in hands-on ways (Pound 2009).

What does this look like in practice?

The outdoor learning environment offers a naturally rich environment for children to initiate their own play, follow their own interests and interact at their own level with nature. Through doing this they develop ideas, knowledge and understanding about the world in which they live. By interacting sensitively with children as they play in the way that Froebel advocated (as gardeners tending plants), practitioners can nurture, enrich and enhance children's self-initiated play to promote learning in an engaging and enjoyable way.

Making mathematical marks

- Provide resources for children to record maps and plans of trails, pathways and journeys.
- Encourage children to record items/patterns/numbers found and collected outside.
- Practise number formation and drawing shapes on a large scale with paints, playground chalks and using water and brushes.

12 | Daily routines

Why daily routines are important

Daily routines are an important part of life within any Early Years setting. These daily occurrences provide a range of learning opportunities. They provide 'real-life', meaningful and purposeful contexts to explore problem solving, number, calculation, shape and pattern. By taking time to tune in to how children operate at these keys times of the day and sensitively leading learning forwards through modelling and open-ended questions, practitioners can gain an all-round knowledge of where children are at mathematically whilst helping them recognise the wonderful world of maths that surrounds them.

Links to other areas of learning

Personal Social and Emotional Development	• Developing confidence and independence as children are involved in regular routines
	• Supporting development of self-care as children learn to look after themselves and contribute to their own wellbeing
	• Helping children learn to deal with change as routines change and vary
	• Encouraging children to work as part of a group, taking turns and sharing, whilst developing a sense of community
	• Helping children to learn about the expectations and boundaries within a setting
	• Providing opportunities to practise dressing and undressing

Communication and Language	• Opportunities to hear and say vocabulary related to daily routine • Providing opportunities for children to talk socially, negotiate and share ideas
Literacy	• Developing early reading skills as children 'read' and respond to simple signs and different text formats • Promoting early mark making opportunities as children indicate their presence, preferences or choices
Understanding the World	• Helping children to develop awareness of time as they become familiar with daily routines and sequence of events • Promoting use of time-related vocabulary • Helping children develop a sense of belonging to a community
Physical Development	• Offering opportunities for children to develop both large-scale and small-scale movements on a daily basis • Helping children develop bodily awareness as they contribute to their own health and wellbeing, making choices about food, drinks and self-care
Expressive Arts and Design	• Providing starting points for role play and small world play • Opportunities to make resources, developing designing and making skills
Mathematics	• Measuring (including time) • Shape and space • Number • Counting • Pattern • Calculating • Problem solving

Key resources

- Sand timers, alarm clocks and cooking timers
- Digital cameras or simple video cameras
- Storage boxes clearly labelled with photos and, where appropriate, numerals
- Self-registration name cards and signs
- Posters illustrating numbers of children allowed to access areas

- Snack area set up as a café
- Mark making materials

Maths web

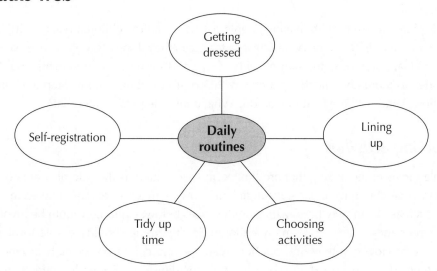

Getting dressed

When children are getting dressed and undressed for role play or PE sessions, or even wrapping up to go outside, there are endless opportunities to talk about sequencing, matching and position. Questions such as: 'What are you going to put on first? Second? Third?' and 'Can you find the other sock/shoe/glove/wellie to match this one?' promote early mathematical skills and vocabulary in a practical way.

Older children can follow a list of pictorial instructions to help them get dressed and undressed. This should include both numerals and pictures illustrating the order. This can be displayed for children to follow when its time to get undressed. Children could make up their list for getting ready for PE or going outside by taking photos at the various stages and sequencing these.

Lining up

Although young children should not spend great deals of time lining up, there are occasions, especially in school, where children are sometimes required to line up for a few minutes. Maximise these spare minutes to promote mathematical learning.

Ask the children to count themselves by counting out loud as you touch them on the head as you move down the line. For example the child at the front shouts out '1', the next child says '2', and so on. When you get to the end of the line, tell the children you are going to count backwards, they simply have to repeat the same number. This provides an opportunity for children to hear counting back and not just counting forwards. For older children this can be extended to incorporate counting in 2s, as the first child whispers 1, whilst the second shouts 2, the third whispers 3, the fourth shouts 4 and so on.

Explore pattern though making people patterns. Can the children make a girl, boy, girl, boy pattern in the line? What other patterns can they think of? Make active patterns such as clap, stamp, clap, stamp, with each child doing an action. This could be extended to more complicated patterns with 3 or 4 repeating actions. Stop the pattern mid-flow. What will the next person do? What about the person after that?

Choosing activities

Popular areas of the setting that are limited in space, such as the role play area or the sand tray, need to have clear signs indicating how many children are allowed in each area, such as '4 can play here' with 4 smiley faces below. Children should be involved in deciding these rules. How many children do they think should be able to play in these areas? How can they find out how many people can fit comfortably around the sand tray? This can be extended further by providing 4 or 5 clearly defined spaces under the sign, where children can attach their photos as they enter the area. This provides a visual way of showing how many children are in the area and also allows other children to see whether there is space for them.

The introduction of sand timers, cooking timers or alarm clocks can provide children with real experiences of time (and the feeling of how long 5, 10 or 15 minutes is). This is particularly useful in popular areas. Children can be shown how to set the timers themselves and be responsible for telling the next person that it's their turn once the timer has rung or beeped.

Tidy up time

Early Years settings by their very nature are a treasure trove of equipment and resources. It is vital that from a young age children are involved in tidying up, developing their sense of responsibility and cooperative skills. Do we make it easy for them to tidy up? Do labels on containers indicate what should go into them and, where appropriate, how many should go in? Children develop not only respect for resources as they make sure the correct amount is replaced, but also number recognition, counting skills and one to one correspondence.

Wooden blocks often come in trolleys or boxes and provide fantastic learning experiences relating to shape and space, not only during playing times, but also at tidy up time. Can the children fit all the bricks back into the box or trolley? Is there a plan they have to follow? Take a photograph of blocks packed into the box and attach this to the lid for children to refer to at tidy up time. Challenge children to create their own plans for friends to follow by printing, drawing or taking a photo.

Self-registration

Many settings encourage children to take their name from one place to another on arrival to indicate their presence. This activity can be developed further by providing simple questions for children to consider once they have collected their name card or photo at the start of the session. The question can change daily and can be linked to favourite programmes, books, characters, food, or anything else you (or the children) can think of. Children can be encouraged to come up with their own questions.

Prepare a set of question cards for the children to think about such as: 'Do you like Peppa Pig?' or 'Do you like bananas?' using a mixture of pictures and words. Laminate 2 sheets of paper, one with 'yes' and a smiley face or tick, and one with 'no' and a sad face or cross. Put these at child height below the chosen question card for the day and ask each child as they enter to take their name card and answer the question, putting it on the yes or no paper. Once everyone is present, look at the yes and no signs. How many people liked Peppa Pig? How many didn't? Which group had more?

Main activity 1

Snack time
You will need:

These suggested resources are based on a small-group, café-style approach, but could be developed for larger groups.

- Table and chairs
- Tablecloth
- Vase with flowers (real, artificial or made by the children)
- Snack menu (see 'Getting started')
- Plates, cups, spoons, knives and forks
- Snack food and drinks
- Bowl of warm soapy water and tea towels (for children to wash up afterwards)

141

Self-registration encourages children to problem solve, make choices, count, sort and handle data.

Getting started

Work with the children to develop a snack menu. What types of food and drink do we have for snack? Make a list of these and use the computer or magazines to find pictures to print out, cut and laminate. Prepare a large piece of paper or card, preferably A3 size, and write Menu at the top and laminate this. Each day the correct pictures can be attached to the menu, clearly showing the children what is on offer and encouraging them to make decisions. Set the snack table with a tablecloth and a vase of flowers. Adults should be involved in snack time with the children, sitting at their level, talking, eating and drinking together.

Snack time activities

Encourage children to set the table each day, working out how many chairs, cups, plates, pieces of cutlery will be needed. Involve children in the preparation of snack; this not only offers opportunities to talk about good hygiene and healthy eating, but also promotes fine motor skills. As children prepare food they can discuss and consider quantities, size, counting and measuring. All too often adults prepare the food and children miss out on a whole wealth of learning and experiences.

Support children to pour drinks for themselves or each other, perhaps using cups with clearly indicated levels marked on the outside. Can they fill it to the right level? Have they got enough? Too much? Not enough? Do all the cups have the same? How many cups can one jug fill before running out?

Prepare cards with children's photographs on, with their names underneath, and put these into a bowl. Prepare a snack register, where children have to put their picture once they have had their snack. This could be extended to develop sorting, as children could put their picture on one side (labelled with a smiley face) if they enjoyed their snack, or on the other side (labelled with a sad face) if they did not. This could lead to discussions about favourite foods.

Offer crackers with a range of toppings. Which ones will they choose? Can they spread the right amount of topping so that the cracker is covered? Which shape cracker will they choose? Round? Square? Rectangle? Provide tomatoes, cucumbers, carrots or other vegetables to make faces, pictures or patterns on the crackers.

What next?

- Encourage children to take on roles at snack time such as setting the table, giving the fruit out, changing the snack menu daily, pouring drinks and washing up.
- Make a simple bar chart using pictures of food or children's photos to show favourite snacks within the group.
- Challenge the children to organise a teddy bears' picnic. How many cups, plates and bowls will they need? How many bottles of drink? How many sandwiches/biscuits, bananas, etc. What types of sandwiches should they make?

Main activity 2

Register time

You will need:

- Registers
- Resources for the children to make their own registers.

Getting started

Whilst it is important to ensure that young children are not sitting for long periods of time, if kept interactive, short and purposeful, register time can be a valuable learning experience. Children can develop the sense of being one of a larger group whilst exploring concepts relating to bigger numbers.

Register time activities

When taking the register, encourage the children to estimate how many will be present. Initially estimates may be large numbers, perhaps in the hundreds or beyond, or equally very small numbers, but as children re-count the same number each day, their estimates will become more realistic. Record these estimates, modelling correct formation and circling the ones that are close and far from the exact number. This could be illustrated on a large number square. Questions such as 'How many children do you think will be here today?', 'How can we find out how many people are/aren't here today?' and 'What would happen if 1, 2 or 3 people came in late or went home early to the dentist?' develop children's calculation and problem solving skills.

Ask the children to put a finger up or make a tally mark for each person who is absent whilst you call the register. Can they tell you how many are away? What would happen if someone arrived late?

Practise counting beyond 10 by counting the number of children present, and model the use of different methods such as all standing up until they are counted or standing them in a line to count, so children can see you solving a problem in different ways.

When children have packed lunches or hot meals in a setting this can extend learning further. They compare which group has more people, consider the difference between the groups and develop one to one correspondence as they realise each lunchbox represents one person. Quite often young children forget to put their lunchboxes on the trolley or in the crate, leading to a real problem to solve: 'How can we have 20 children saying they are having packed lunch but only 19 boxes? What could have happened? How can we solve the problem?'

What next?

- Keep a daily record of how many packed lunches/hot dinners there were each day. Compare the days: which day had the most/least packed lunches or hot dinners? Why did so many children have hot dinner on a particular day?

- Set up a school role play area with registers for the children to play with. Encourage the children to write their own friends' names by having displays of photos and name cards for them to refer to.

- Provide a box of buttons, shells or conkers and explain to the children that as they enter the classroom they have to take one and put it into a container. Before starting the register ask the children to estimate how many things will be in the jar. After the register and counting the children, count the conkers/ shells or buttons and see if the number matches. Did anyone forget to put one in the jar? Extend this by providing different-coloured beads/cubes to represent packed lunches/hot dinners and two jars. Which one has more or fewer?

Daily routines such as looking at a calendar offer children the opportunity to use vocabulary related to the passing of time, days of the week, months of the year, ordinal numbers and simple data handling.

Look, listen and note

- Are children able to count irregular arrangements of objects? Which methods do they use to help them count?
- How are they using their developing ideas to solve real-life problems?
- Do they recognise any numerals and how do they attempt to represent these?
- Do they recognise and talk about shapes and patterns in their environment?
- Are they able to talk about how they sort and arrange items?

? Key questions

- What do you think you might need to do here?
- How many do you think there are going to be?
- How much do you think you will need?
- I wonder what would happen if . . .
- Can you think of another way of doing that?

Key vocabulary

Counting: Number, zero, one, two, three…ten and beyond, how many…? guess how many, estimate, nearly, too many, too few

Calculating: Add, more, less, altogether, one more, two more, take away, one less, two less, most, least

Solving problems: Count, sort, match, same, different, find out

Measuring: Full, empty, how much, not enough, too much, too little

Time: How long, minutes, timer, clock, day, morning, afternoon, first, next, after, before

Health and safety

- If children are using tools independently to cut snack foods, adults must ensure that they are taught to use them safely, alerted to the possible dangers and supervised.

- Any spillages must be mopped up immediately when pouring drinks to avoid slips, trips and falls.
- Adults need to be aware of food allergies in relation to snack times to ensure that the food offered is appropriate.

📖 Useful stories and rhymes

Tidy Titch (Pat Hutchins, Red Fox, 1993)
This book links to tidy up time and organising spaces.

Here we go round the mulberry bush (Traditional rhyme)
This rhyme could be linked to the various stages of getting dressed, getting ready for the garden, tidying up or any other routine.

How Do I Put It On? (Shigeo Watanbe, Red Fox, 1993)
Links to dressing up and putting clothes on the right way.

Oliver's Vegetables (Vivian French and Alison Bartlett, Hodder Children's Books, 1995)

Oliver's Fruit Salad (Vivian French and Alison Bartlett, Hodder Children's Books, 1998)

Oliver's Milkshake (Vivian French and Alison Bartlett, Hodder Children's Books, 2000)
Link to healthy eating, fruit, vegetables and milk, and would support work on counting, sorting and size.

Links to theory

HighScope

The HighScope approach is underpinned by 5 principles, illustrated in a Wheel of Learning. One aspect of the wheel is 'Daily routine'. HighScope advocates a consistent routine-based day, where children develop independence and a sense of security, enabling them to embrace learning and new experiences feeling confident. Large-group times are used to develop a sense of community whilst small-group times, individual time, and a balance of child-led and adult-led learning are also important parts of the HighScope ethos. Everyday occurrences such as tidy up time and snack time are viewed as valuable learning experiences, providing opportunities for adults and children to spend quality time together (Holt 2007).

In his *Independent Review of Mathematics Teaching in Early Years Settings and Primary Schools* (2008), Sir Peter Williams concluded that everyday routines needed to be maximised by effective practitioners who interact and talk mathematically with children to promote mathematical learning.

What does this look like in practice?

It is vital that routines are developed with the children and in response to their needs. Practitioners need to recognise the potential of the routines within their setting and use them effectively as a valuable part of everyday learning. By interacting with children, modelling appropriate mathematical language and being 'maths role models', practitioners can help children to develop their mathematical knowledge, skills and understanding. When children encounter problems to solve, numbers, shapes and patterns as part of their daily routines, it promotes a sense that maths is everywhere and important in their lives.

Making mathematical marks

- Provide resources for children to make their own lists, registers and signs.
- Encourage children to find ways to record what they have done.
- Model using tallies to solve simple problems (numbers of lunches, favourite snacks).
- Challenge children to find out how many people are present each day and finds ways to show this.

Bibliography

Aubrey, C. and Dahl, S. (2008) *A Review of the Evidence on the Use of ICT in the Early Years Foundation Stage*, BECTA. Online. Available http://dera.ioe.ac.uk/1631/2/becta_2008_eyfsreview_report.pdf (accessed 13 May 2011).

Bruce, T. (2004) *Developing Learning in Early Childhood*, London: Paul Chapman Publishing.

Cooney, W., Cross, C. and Trunk, B. (1993) *From Plato to Piaget: The Greatest Educational Theorists from across the Centuries and Around the World*, Lanham, MD: University Press of America.

DCSF (2008) *Early Years Foundation Stage*, Nottingham: DCSF Publications.

Desforges, C. (2003) *The Impact of Parental Involvement, Parental Support and Family Education on Pupil Achievement and Adjustment*, DfES Research Report. Online. Available www.bgfl.org/bgfl/custom/files_uploaded/uploaded_resources/18617/Desforges.pdf (accessed 12 May 2011).

DFEE (2000) *Mathematical vocabulary*, DFEE Publications. Online. Available http://webarchive.nationalarchives.gov.uk/20110202093118/http:/nationalstrategies.standards.dcsf.gov.uk/node/84996 (accessed 1 November 2011).

DfES (2003) *The Impact of Parental Involvement on Children's Education*, Online. Available www.education.gov.uk/publications/eOrderingDownload/DfES0645200MIG2529.pdf (accessed 12 May 2011).

Holt, N. (2007) *Bringing the High/Scope Approach to Your Early Years Practice*, London: Routledge.

Pound, L. (2005) *How Children Learn*, London: Practical Pre-School Books.

Pound, L. (2009) *How Children Learn 3: Contemporary Thinking and Theorists*, London: Practical Pre-School Books.

Sutherland, M. (1988) *Theory of Education*, Harlow: Longman.

Tickell, C. (2011) *The Early Years: Foundation for Life, Health and Learning: An Independent Report on the Early Years Foundation Stage to Her Majesty's Government.* Online. Available http://media.education.gov.uk/ MediaFiles/B/1/5/%7BB15EFF0D-A4DF-4294-93A1-1E1B88C13F68%7DTickell%20review.pdf (accessed 7 April 2011).

Williams, P. (2008), *Independent Review of Mathematics Teaching in Early Years Settings and Primary Schools, Final Report*, Nottingham: DCSF Publications.